REFLECTIONS ON ECONOMIC DEVELOPMENT

Toward a New Latin American Consensus

ENRIQUE V. IGLESIAS

Published by the Inter-American Development Bank
Distributed by The Johns Hopkins University Press

Washington, D.C.
1992

The views and opinions expressed in this publication are those of the author and do not necessarily reflect the official position of the Inter-American Development Bank.

Reflections on Economic Development
Toward a New Latin American Consensus

© Copyright 1992 by the Inter-American Development Bank.

Inter-American Development Bank
1300 New York Avenue, N.W.
Washington, D.C. 20577

Distributed by
The Johns Hopkins University Press
701 West 40th Street
Baltimore, MD 21211

ISBN: 0-940602-52-0

A little over twenty years ago Felipe Herrera, the first president of the Inter-American Development Bank, asked Dr. Raúl Prebisch to prepare a report on the problems, experiences and prospects of economic and social development in Latin America. It was my honor at the time to assist Dr. Prebisch in the preparation of this study, which was entitled *Change and Development: Latin America's Great Task*. The Report was submitted to the meeting of the Board of Governors held in April 1970 in Punta del Este, Uruguay. As Mr. Herrera pointed out in the preface to the published version of the Report, many of the statements and discussions in this meeting were aimed at evaluating the Report's findings.

Two decades later, it seemed appropriate to me to repeat this experiment and to analyze the challenges, characteristics and possible solutions of the major development problems in the region, taking into account the changes that have occurred in the last twenty years. It also seemed appropriate to submit these reflections to the Governors and Executive Directors of the Inter-American Development Bank and the Inter-American Investment Corporation at the annual meeting to be held in Santo Domingo in April of this year.

In his preface to the edition of the Report published by the Fondo de Cultura Económica in 1970, Felipe Herrera, referring to some of the essential characteristics of this document, wrote: "Dr. Prebisch's focus transcended and enhanced the main objectives we initially had in sight. The thrust of the analysis was not the problem of financing in itself, but rather the evaluation of overall development strategies. In this way, external financial cooperation became one aspect of a much broader view of the problems of Latin America."

In preparing this analysis, I was guided by the same purpose. It is not my intention here to reflect on what the Bank does, but rather to examine the economic experience of Latin America and the principal options available to it. Not only is the IDB a unique vantage point for such an undertaking, it also has the responsibility to carry out this examination on an ongoing basis in order to have constant access to the information needed to orient its policies and operations. Of course, the Bank is fully capable of accomplishing this examination, so this observation is made on a purely personal basis, as part of the ineluctable responsibility of its president to formulate his own vision of the context in which the institution functions.

The above does not mean, however, that this is merely an individual reflection, since I was aided in the preparation of this document by numerous individuals and experiences. Among these, special mention should be made of the seminar organized by the IDB in November of last year, entitled "Latin American Thought: Past, Present and Future," in which a retrospective of the life of Raúl Prebisch was the inspiration for putting forward ideas about the formulation of a new development strategy for the 1990s. The meeting was attended by some of the most distinguished specialists in the field of economic development, for whose contributions and comments I am especially grateful.

Nonetheless, this document is not an addendum to the analysis we conducted in 1970 with Dr. Prebisch, nor is it an attempt to determine to what extent his most important ideas were borne out in the subsequent economic growth of Latin America. The economic environment of both the world and Latin America has changed so much since then that many of the key variables we used in those days are no longer as important as they once were, or their whole nature has changed. What I originally intended was to examine the economic growth of Latin America from the perspective of its own history and to review the current discussion of the topic of development as objectively and with as broad a perspective as possible.

Naturally, these comments are not confined to the experience of Latin America but rather attempt to place it within the changing context of international economic policy. Shortly after attending a seminar on the private sector recently organized by the IDB, a prominent Latin American businessman wrote to me to say that one of the most common mistakes in the economic thinking of the region in the past was to concentrate too heavily on our own reality and not to look at the "wide world" it is a part of. This document takes heed of that comment in the dual sense of looking beyond both the Bank and the region, in an effort to understand the origins of the trends that affect us most directly. To do so, it was inevitable that consideration be given not only to economic factors but also to social and political factors, since recent experience reaffirms that events in the world and in Latin America are increasingly influenced by all three.

Enrique V. Iglesias
Washington, D.C.
March 1992

Contents

CHAPTER VI

The international insertion of the region

CHAPTER VII

Latin America at the time of the Prebisch Report

Chapter I

The economy of Latin America in the postwar era

The Report prepared by Dr. Raúl Prebisch in 1970, *Change and Development: Latin America's Great Task*, is a distillation and updating of the thinking of both the author and a large group of collaborators, which contains an incisive analysis of the problems and prospects of Latin American development at that point in time. It is therefore an excellent point of reference for reflecting, twenty years later and in the same institution where the Report was written, on what has happened in the region in the last two decades and on the confusing and critical, yet stimulating period in which we live. It also provides a unique vantage point from which to compare the principal stages of Latin American development.

A historic retrospective

The characteristics, difficulties and requirements of development in Latin America cannot be understood without a proper historical perspective. This being the case, the period in which the Report was written cannot be fully comprehended without taking into account the fight for development that the countries of the region waged in the preceding twenty years, just as it is impossible to understand today's complex and turbulent situation, or the ways in which it differs from that earlier time, without carefully analyzing the events of the twenty years following the publication of the Report.

Latin America entered the second half of the twentieth century in a state of economic and social underdevelopment, a product of its historical heritage that was made worse by the prolonged period of international economic dissolution caused by the Great Depression of the 1930s and the Second World War. This was a group of vulnerable, open economies that exported mostly raw materials and that was committed to an outward-oriented growth strategy, the normal development of which had been severely curtailed by the aforementioned world events. At the end of the war, these countries struggled to reenter the world economy and to do so

Latin America's entry into the postwar era

in a better position than before. These ambitions clashed with the prevailing external conditions.

At the time, the efforts of the international community, led by the United States, were focused, first, on containing Soviet expansion; second, on promoting a process of global economic recovery after so many years of stagnation and conflict; and third, on the reconstruction of countries devastated by the war. The fact that the Latin American countries were not high on the list of priorities made it inadvisable for them to base their growth strategies on participation in the world economy and access to international markets, which forced them instead to try various domestic growth strategies. Thus, the period extending from the end of the Second World War to the beginning of the 1970s was characterized by the subordination of economic and social development interests to the preservation of hemispheric security in the context of the Cold War, the apparent dependence of the countries of the region on the United States, with a sharp contraction in their foreign relations within the hemisphere, and their ongoing struggle to convince their superpower neighbor of the need to shift the focus of their mutual relations from hemispheric security to cooperation for development. It was only in the early seventies that this began to happen.

In the years following the Second World War, the countries of Latin America—many of which, motivated by the double stimulus of their own internal dynamic and the international conditions created by the war, had initiated development and industrialization processes at various times and with various objectives in sight—had already begun to advance their claims in the economic and social field, and were seeing increasingly less reason for contributing to the defense efforts of the United States. The countries advanced their claims in the arena within which these relations had always evolved: the inter-American system. These objectives were thwarted by the United States' insistence on giving top priority to hemispheric security.

This standoff is clearly reflected in the various results achieved in the Rio de Janeiro Conference held in 1947, at which the Inter-American Treaty of Reciprocal Assistance was signed, and in the IX American International Conference held in Bogota in 1948, at which the Organization of American States (OAS) was founded. The Rio Treaty fulfilled the agreements concluded in 1945 at the Inter-American Conference on War and Peace, held in Chapultepec, Mexico, for the purpose of creating a means of joint defense against any form of aggression, whether from within or from outside the continent, the fear at the time being that such aggression would come from the Communist bloc. At the Bogota Conference the OAS Charter was approved,[1] extending to the political and legal fields the means of cooperation provided for by the Rio Treaty in the military sphere, but Latin American efforts to project this cooperation to economic and social matters were rejected.

This difference in outlook characterized inter-American relations for the next ten years. Throughout this period, the Latin American countries took every opportunity to try to persuade the United States to implement a financial cooperation program to promote their processes of economic and social development, but without success. Perhaps the most important turning point in these years was the Caracas Conference of 1954.

It should be noted that before this, an important event had taken place outside the hemisphere with the creation of the Economic Commission for Latin America (ECLA). In 1947 a group of Latin American delegations to the United Nations Economic and Social Council, in which the Chilean delegation played a very prominent role, proposed the creation of a permanent regional economic commission within the global organization. Apparently, this proposal conflicted with certain of the organization's principles and priorities; on the one hand because of its international character and, on the other, because of the importance ascribed at the time to the problems of peace and international security. To overcome these objections, it was necessary to prepare a careful defense of the proposal.

The creation of ECLA

The main thesis of the argument stressed the fact that the Latin American countries were forced to sell their exports—consisting overwhelmingly of raw materials—at ever lower prices, and to buy increasingly expensive equipment, inputs and industrial goods needed to renovate their economic infrastructure and further their development. It was also emphasized that having joined the war effort with the other allies, the region had been required to sell its products at controlled prices, whereas it now had to replace its equipment in a free market with high prices. The difficulty posed by the ecumenical nature of the United Nations was overcome by the agreement of the United States, France and other industrialized countries to join the new regional economic commission, thus giving it a much broader scope. The creation of ECLA was probably the first

---

[1] This was accomplished despite the fact that the delegates from the various countries were virtual prisoners in the Hotel Tequendama due to the bloody social disturbances caused by the assassination of the populist leader Jorge Eliecer Gaitán.

step taken by the international community to focus attention on the economic and social development problems of the least developed countries within the ambit of the United Nations—in this case referring to Latin America—thus establishing a precedent for creating additional economic commissions in other regions of the developing world.[2] It also served as a point of reference, as explained below, for developing a distinctly Latin American approach to economics.

Another step forward was taken, this time within Latin America, at the abovementioned Caracas Meeting, although it ultimately proved to be tentative and incomplete. In 1954 the reform government of Juan José Arévalo in Guatemala was replaced by the more radical government of Jacobo Arbenz, who, unlike his predecessor, included a number of Communist representatives in his administration. Given the ruling perception at the time, this could be viewed as a threat to the security of the hemisphere. The United States, which is where this perception came from, decided it had to intervene, but it wanted to do so under cover of the regional joint security procedures established by the Rio Treaty. To achieve this goal, it convoked the Caracas Conference, at which the United States was represented by its Secretary of State, John Foster Dulles. The conference's interpretation of the treaty was that a government such as Guatemala's was vulnerable to foreign infiltration and posed a threat to the security of the hemisphere, which justified intervention. A number of Latin American countries made their accession to this interpretation conditional upon an agreement to convoke within the coming months a hemispheric economic conference similar to the one held in Bogota six years earlier. This meeting was held in Quitandinha, Brazil, in November and December of 1954 and was sponsored by the Inter-American Economic and Social Council (ECOSOC) of the OAS.

The Latin American countries prepared for this conference swiftly and in great earnest. They formed a commission that met at ECLA in the months preceding the conference under the leadership of Dr. Raúl Prebisch. Eduardo Frei presided over the meetings and Carlos Lleras Restrepo served as Executive Secretary.

This enabled the Latin American countries to go to the meeting with a coherent set of ideas and proposals concerning the

Invitation to an economic conference

Events at the Quitandinha meeting

---

[2] The only commissions functioning at this time were the European and Middle Eastern commissions, which, created to aid in the reconstruction of those areas affected by the war, were basically temporary.

appropriate design of a program for cooperation on development in the hemisphere, prepared by a representative group of Latin American leaders. This action plan, which was actually based on the analysis of central and peripheral relations undertaken by ECLA five years earlier, basically proposed the conclusion of agreements to stabilize the prices of commodities, which constituted the bulk of the Latin American countries' exports, and the establishment of an Inter-American Development Fund, which, years later, became a reality with the creation of the IDB. The U.S. delegation was headed by the Secretary of the Treasury, George Humphrey, who repeated the observations made on various occasions in hemispheric conferences that the United States did not have the public funds to finance a program of this type, that the country had other priorities also, that in general there were no development projects in the region that could not be financed due to a lack of resources and that, in any case, the foreign resources necessary to supplement Latin American development financing should come from the private sector.

The ideas put forward in the Quitandinha meeting were not forgotten, but they could not be brought up again until another opportunity presented itself, which occurred in 1958 during a trip to a number of Latin American countries by the Vice President of the United States, Richard Nixon. The cool reception and open hostility he encountered in some of the countries he visited made the United States government aware for the first time of the deep political, economic and social unrest in the region. In the following months the U.S. government deployed an active presence in Latin America, culminating with a meeting between the U.S. Secretary of State, John Foster Dulles, and the President of Brazil, Juscelino Kubitschek. The Brazilian president proposed a broad program for cooperation on the economic and social development of the Latin American countries, which he suggested be called the Pan-American Operation. This proposal was ultimately accepted.

The Pan-American Operation

Thus, after a decade of negotiations, a consensus was reached between the United States and the countries of Latin America to shift the focus of their reciprocal relations from military security to cooperation for development.

After the launching of the Pan-American Operation in August 1958, it was decided that this proposal would be studied in a meeting of the ministers of foreign relations of all the countries in the hemisphere, to be held in Washington in September of that year. Symbolically, this meeting was preceded by an announcement in a special meeting of ECOSOC by the Under-Secretary of the United States Treasury, Douglas Dillon, that his country was prepared to

The Washington meeting: Birth of the IDB

participate in a regional financial organization—which later became the IDB—as well as to take the necessary steps to accede to the International Coffee Agreement, which the U.S. government had previously opposed because of its stance against price stabilization agreements involving commodities, which it considered a tool of market intervention. The meeting established the "Committee of 21," consisting of representatives from all the member countries of the inter-American system, to implement these agreements. Encouraged by the impact these measures had in Latin America, in November of that year President Eisenhower visited Argentina, Brazil, Chile and Uruguay, where he was given a warm welcome.

In early January 1959, forces led by Fidel Castro entered Havana. A short time later, Commander Castro attended the Second Plenary Session of the Committee of 21 in Buenos Aires, which created great expectations. In his speech, he affirmed that the political instability of Latin America was due not to the Soviet threat but to underdevelopment, and that the countries of Latin America did not want to become a battlefield for world political conflicts. At this meeting Castro proposed that the United States provide $30 billion to promote the development of the Latin American countries. Although this figure was considered exorbitant by the representative of the United States (the Undersecretary of State for Inter-American Affairs, Roy Rubotton), it is fairly close to what was later granted to the Alliance for Progress. It is possible that the success of the revolutionary forces in Cuba had some effect on the presidential campaign taking shape in the United States and helped to raise the priority assigned to Latin American affairs.

The position taken at the close of the Eisenhower administration laid the foundation for a new U.S. policy toward Latin America. But the inspiration, the philosophy and the orchestration of the new strategy were the work of President John F. Kennedy. The new U.S. president took a personal interest in Latin America. During his campaign for office, in which he ran against Nixon, the disinformation passed back and forth between the Eisenhower administration and Cuba was vividly present in the minds of the U.S. public, as well as in the campaign itself. After his election, Kennedy organized a series of working groups to prepare policy recommendations concerning the major topics the new government should address. One of these was a group for Latin America. To head this group Kennedy appointed Adolph Berle, a distinguished lawyer, diplomat and politician whose career stretched back to the First World War and whose law firm had been visited by prominent Latin Americans. Among those who worked with him were Lincoln Gordon and

Richard Goodwin. Berle surrounded himself with U.S. academics who specialized in Latin America. This group had a "Latin American connection" on at least three levels. The first consisted of a group of Puerto Rican reformists headed by the governor of the island, Luis Muñoz Marín. This group in turn had close ties to the leaders of the largest Latin American progressive parties, such as José Figueres in Costa Rica and Rómulo Betancourt in Venezuela. Lastly, around this time, an outstanding regional technocracy had coalesced, headed by Raúl Prebisch of ECLA, Felipe Herrera of the IDB and Jorge Sol Castellanos, the Executive Secretary of ECOSOC. This facilitated a fluid exchange of ideas among these individuals and institutions, with the result that a proposal was made to President Kennedy, which he made his own and which he announced in a speech delivered March 13, 1961, to the Inter-American Press Society. His proposals, which he included within the concept of an "Alliance for Progress" between the two halves of the hemisphere, focused direct attention for the first time on the economic and social development problems of Latin America and incorporated, also for the first time, most of the ideas advanced by a representative and united team of Latin American leaders.

The program of the Alliance for Progress included:

a)   a decade of "maximum effort," during which the United States would allocate $20 billion to aid development in Latin America;

Proposals of the Alliance for Progress

b)   support for the industrialization of the region and the diversification of its imports;

c)   modernization of the agricultural sector and the implementation of agrarian reforms;

d)   expansion of the physical infrastructure of the Latin American countries: energy, transportation and communications;

e)   promotion of social development: housing, health and education;

f)   modernization of the universities;

g)   creation of scientific and technological development systems;

h)   establishment of national planning offices;

i)   support for regional integration; and

j)   study, on a case-by-case basis, of measures to stabilize the prices of Latin America's primary exports.

One of the most interesting aspects of the Alliance for Progress was the complex institutional framework created to provide for multilateral management of a substantial portion of the program's funds. It is true that a proposal to create a multilateral structure authorized to administer this program was rejected in Punta del Este, possibly because both the United States and the Latin American countries suspected, for different reasons, that such multilateralism would limit the political discretion with which the donor country could allocate the resources of the Alliance and would restrict the Latin American countries' freedom to use them as they saw fit. Nevertheless, the United States had already agreed to contribute $500 million to a Social Progress Trust Fund, which was later placed under the administration of the IDB. After Punta del Este, a list of nine experts—technical, not political—was drawn up, which was to have a significant impact on the allocation of the Fund's resources. After two years of operations, and based on the experience to date, the list of nine proposed the creation of what would later become the Inter-American Committee on the Alliance for Progress (ICAP), consisting of representatives from all the countries. Although ICAP officially functioned within the framework of the OAS, it enjoyed wide latitude in the exercise of its authority to evaluate the development programs of the Latin American countries and their external financing requirements. It should be noted that although the IDB had multilateral agencies of its own to allocate its resources, a considerable portion of the funds of the Alliance for Progress was channeled through other agencies such as the AID. ICAP, as an objective, multilateral organization responsible for allocating the resources and coordinating the policies of international cooperation, was a new experience, possibly not repeated since.

The Alliance for Progress period was one in which the Latin American countries, after tremendous efforts, succeeded in shifting the focus of international relations from the military to the economic sphere. It was also an unprecedented experience in terms of reconciling the interests of both the Latin American countries and the United States. Certain restrictions notwithstanding, it was also probably one of those times when the elusive search for multilateralism found a more concrete expression in the inter-American environment. It is worth repeating that most of the external economic relations of the Latin American countries at this time were concentrated in the hemisphere.

Despite the positive results of the Alliance for Progress, toward the end of the sixties it had lost its original momentum and had been rendered ineffective by a variety of circumstances. First, the main premise on which this program was based—the existence of a sort of natural harmony of interests between the United States and Latin America which, in fact, was first expressed in the consensus of ideas from which this program emerged—was invalidated by the fact that the governments that came to power in various Latin American countries in the mid-sixties had a more independent or more nationalistic viewpoint than that of previous governments. Second, the quantitative goals of the Alliance for Progress, which were initially defined in statistical terms, failed to take into account the existence of a "vicious cycle of development," especially its early stages, wherein the successes of a given stage created greater demands and pressures as a consequence of the heightened expectations these same successes raised. Finally, the political conditions that formed the basis of the hemispheric consensus that led to the creation of the Alliance also changed with the January 1969 inauguration of President Richard Nixon, whose foreign policy reverted to a global perspective with no room for the specific interests of particular regions such as Latin America, and with the end of the basic similarity of the political regimes and the moderately reformist development strategies of the Latin American countries that had endorsed this program.

These changes led the President of the IDB, Felipe Herrera, to ask Raúl Prebisch to prepare a special report on the development prospects of the region at that point in time.

The Latin American development model

Added to the prevailing conditions in Latin America in the 1930s and the difficulties it experienced in attempting to gain a foothold in a world economy powered by an accelerated process of industrial development were the limitations created by the depression early in the decade and the war at its end, leading to the adoption of a series of unavoidable and/or pragmatic measures, which were later condensed into a series of policy orientations that were then used in the formulation of a Latin American development strategy or model. This model was largely attributed to ECLA. The chronology and origin of these measures make it debatable whether, as was generally believed, they constituted a true model and whether that was the actual intention. It is also debatable whether these strategies were proposed by ECLA alone. What this organization did, thanks to the intellectual leadership of Raúl Prebisch, was to develop a rational synthesis of these policies and to explain, perhaps for the first time, the perceptions and assumptions on which they were based, thus

The intellectual leadership of ECLA

enabling the countries to apply them in a more coherent manner than they had in the past. A point that should not be overlooked in this connection is that a number of countries, responding to the internal and external circumstances discussed above, adopted strategies of this type as a practical matter prior to the creation of ECLA, as witnessed by the fact that in the 1930s, the relatively more advanced countries of the region had already created institutions to promote these policies, including *Nacional Financiera* in Mexico and *Corporación de Fomento de la Producción* in Chile. In any case, although no one claimed that they constituted a model strictly speaking, the ideas that inspired the development policies of Latin America prior to the Prebisch Report are part of a school of economic thought that came to be known as "structuralist."

The model's external assumptions

This school of thought held a number of assumptions concerning the external environment. The first was that Latin America's role in the international division of labor tended to make it a natural exporter of raw materials and an importer of the capital assets and manufactured goods it needed to further its development process and to satisfy its growing social aspirations. Another assumption was that because of Engel's Law and the replacement of natural resources with synthetic products, the terms of trade tended systematically toward the stagnation and fall of the prices of raw materials and the rise of prices of manufactured goods. A basic corollary of these two assumptions was the existence of chronic imbalances in the external accounts of the Latin American countries. Since this was a group of developing countries, domestic savings were small by definition, which gave rise to the theory of two gaps, trade and savings, which were considered the two major obstacles to the processes of investment and economic growth.

The model's internal assumptions

These ideas also encompassed a series of assumptions concerning the internal situation, including the reluctance of the industrial sector to expand and compete on its own because of its incipient character and the narrowness of its markets, which deprived it of access to economies of scale and the technological advances upon which the industrial development of the more advanced countries was based; the relative weight of the agricultural sector and its considerable underdevelopment, due chiefly to the existing land-holding systems; the economic and social disparities between the country and the city, between blue and white collar workers in the latter, and between industrial and marginal workers; the lack of institutional development; and the inability to mobilize domestic resources.

Both types of assumptions led to the same basic prescription: industrialization seemed the best route. First, because it could change Latin America's share in the international division of labor and correct the trend of its terms of trade, and, second, because it could productively absorb the redundant work force in rural areas, increase productivity, accelerate the growth of the gross domestic product and ameliorate income distribution. Naturally, in light of the conditions to which the above assumptions refer, this industrialization process could not be spontaneous but would require planning and would have to replace imports.

A basic prescription: import substitution

This line of thinking evolved along empirical and historical lines. Accordingly, two stages can be distinguished in the process of Latin American development, characterized in the first instance by the emergence and growth of primary-exporter economies and, in the second, by import substitution. In the terminology developed by ECLA, the two stages were, respectively, "outward-oriented" development and "inward-oriented" development.

In the first stage, which stretches from the closing decades of the last century to the Great Depression of the 1930s, the most dynamic sectors of the Latin American economies were part of the international economic system taking shape as capitalism spread, under the leadership first of Great Britain and then of the United States. The driving force behind the growth of the Latin American economies at the time was external demand, spurred by the growth of shipping. The export of capital from Europe to certain peripheral regions in the downward phase of the third Kondratieff wave, between the Franco-Prussian War and the mid-1890s, and the growing demand for raw materials and food at the beginning of the next wave, strengthened the role of this external force. Under its influence, exports of Latin American raw materials grew rapidly, attracting domestic and foreign investments, utilizing modern technology, promoting the creation of an institutional, financial and physical infrastructure, putting the region's business skills to the test and generating employment. The growth of international trade also raised geographic income, made it possible to increase exports and to orient them primarily toward satisfying the needs of high income groups, increased fiscal resources and encouraged the formation of an incipient middle class. The Latin American economies opened to the exterior to the point that, as explained below in the discussion of the theory of dependency, their export sectors became actual segments of the industrialized countries' economic frontier.

From "outward-oriented" to "inward-oriented" development

Nevertheless, the growth of demand for raw materials was uneven and each crisis in the industrial centers caused a contraction

11

of this demand and of international credits, which had the effect of increasing the vulnerability of the Latin American economies. The lesson provided by the Great Depression was unequivocal. The Latin American governments improvised measures to keep the export sector functioning and to sustain employment levels. They initiated exchange controls, devalued currencies, most of them suspended external debt payments and "practiced Keynesianism without knowing it." The prices for imported products rose faster than for domestic products, and the funds diverted from the export sector were used to produce goods that were previously imported, marking the beginning of unplanned industrialization. In the thirties and forties, to replace unavailable or more expensive imports, Latin America expanded its import substitution industry and plants worked at maximum capacity. Thus, just as it has been said that there was an urbanization process in Latin America without industrialization, it can also be said that in this period there was an industrialization process in the region without industrial policies. But toward the end of the period, governments became aware that industrialization was the route the region had to take if it wanted to limit its external vulnerability, gradually internalize the driving forces of its economic growth and create a situation where, of all the goods available to the community, the percentage from abroad was smaller than in the past. Nevertheless, at the same time, it was also recognized that this route did not promote exports and, therefore, the external fiscal imbalance persisted. The analyses of ECLA and of Dr. Prebisch were based on this experience. "It is a well-known fact," he said with his characteristic emphasis, "that by industrializing, the Latin American countries tend to grow faster than their exports."[3]

Raúl Prebisch interpreted and systematized these perceptions by asserting that the route to Latin American development was basically through industrialization, that this process had to be planned, and that it had to be based on substitution policies aimed at locally producing a growing range of goods that were previously imported, with a moderate degree of protection such as that recommended a century earlier for industry, which was then in its infancy. In fact, in his early writings, Prebisch referred to a tariff of roughly 10 percent, which was quickly exceeded with the establishment of a high level of protection in specific sectors such as the automotive industry and others.

---

[3]   R. Prebisch, *Problemas teóricos y prácticos del crecimiento económico*, United Nations, 1952, p. 12.

"My proposed development policy," Prebisch wrote in a retrospective summary of his economic thought, "was oriented toward the establishment of a new pattern of development which would make it possible to overcome the limitations of the previous pattern. This new form of development would have industrialization as its main objective. In reality, my policy proposal sought to provide theoretical justification for the industrialization policy which was already being followed (especially by the large countries of Latin America), to encourage the others to follow it too, and to provide all of them with an orderly strategy for carrying this out. This task was by no means easy, because the recovery of the international economic order after the Second World War and the expansion of exports caused a resurgence of the champions of outward-oriented development and the criticism of industrialization of the periphery."[4]

The last sentence seems to confirm some of the criticism leveled against Prebisch's thinking, in the sense that it was excessively pessimistic about the foreign market. "The postwar period saw actual improvement in the terms of trade for many countries and favorable prospects for exports. Thus it was necessary to invoke long-term and inevitable trends, and normative arguments to counteract the immediate force of market signals."[5] Nevertheless, it is important not to underestimate the slowness of the recovery of the commercial and institutional financial markets, the trend toward the interdependence of markets of the more developed countries through a dynamic process of transnationalization, and the even greater slowness with which its effects benefited the countries of Latin America, which were largely excluded from this process for a long time.

The economic history of Latin America cannot be reconstructed solely on an intellectual basis, but must also include realities. The force of Prebisch's ideas was due to two inseparable factors: his ability to mold them into a powerful combination of concepts, institutions and policies,[6] and their immediate and complete acceptance by the governments. In fact, Raúl Prebisch was able to disseminate his forceful ideas in Latin America through ECLA and worldwide

A pessimistic view of the foreign market

The grounding in reality of Prebisch's intellectual development

---

[4] R. Prebisch, "Five Stages in my Thinking on Development," in G.M. Meier and D. Seers, *Pioneers in Development*, a World Bank Publication, Oxford University Press, 1984, p. 177.

[5] A. Fishlow, "Comment," in Meier and Seers, op cit., p. 193.

[6] An ability demonstrated by E.J. Dosman and D. Pollock in "Raúl Prebisch, 1901-1971: The Continuing Quest," prepared for the conference "Latin-American Economic Thought: Past, Present and Future," organized by the IDB, Washington, D.C., November 14 and 15, 1991.

through UNCTAD. "In both institutions, this economist wielded an unmistakable charismatic power, consistent with the early stages of an organization, which, according to Webster, qualified as a 'sect.' When these transnational organizations reached the 'ecclesiastical,' technobureaucratic stage, Prebisch abandoned them or else exercised a personal influence that sidestepped the bureaucratic channels. Whether as a 'sect' or as a 'church,' these institutions made Prebisch an 'armed prophet': he had a message, resources and a forum duly legitimized by the governments, the formal source of authority."[7] The governments of Latin America played a decisive role in the establishment and consolidation of ECLA, from which the thinking of Prebisch was initially disseminated. The opposition to the creation of ECLA was overcome only with the active support of Cuba, Chile, Peru and Venezuela, which were later joined by most of the other countries of the region, including Brazil and Mexico. Brazil played a decisive role in the conversion of ECLA into a permanent organization, three years later, by hosting the sessions on this subject and supporting the initiative.[8]

The ability to change

Another reason for the interpretative value of Prebisch's thinking was his ability to change the course of his ideas. Hodara, in the book cited above, sets forth Prebisch's ideas in non-chronological order, beginning with his analysis of peripheral capitalism, the crisis of the centers and the social distribution of the surplus. He then discusses his early comments on the external and internal obstacles to growth, the center-periphery relationship, inward-oriented development, planning and economic integration. The author's reason for this is to avoid two optical illusions. "[The first] is that Prebisch's theses followed a strict, incremental order, as observed in the curvilinear growth of a discipline. It is my belief that these opinions were instead reactions to changing realities and were developed as a result of 'mandates' issued by the governments. Prebisch's interpretative apparatus adapted itself creatively to these government and institutional pronouncements; it was activated more by exogenous variables than by internal, imminent growth....The second illusion refers to the teleological purpose. It is incorrect to suggest that Prebisch's early ideas led inevitably to the more recent ones. Unforeseeable

---

[7] J. Hodara, *Prebisch y la CEPAL: Sustancia, trayectoria y contexto institucional,* El Colegio de México, 1987, p. 21.

[8] See H. Santa Cruz, *Cooperar o perecer: El dilema de la comunidad mundial,* Volume I, Buenos Aires, GEL, 1984, and C. Furtado, *La fantasía organizada,* Buenos Aires, EUDEBA, 1987.

personal and circumstantial factors influenced this isolation."[9] Actually, Prebisch's leadership was based not only on his enormous intellectual depth but also his lively sense of history and consistent ability to evaluate and to criticize. In his later writings, Prebisch was one of the first critics of the limitations of import substitution and the exaggerations of protectionism. From the late 1950s onward, there was a growing emphasis in his work, especially through UNCTAD, on the need to expand and diversify exports, to create a greater economic capacity for this expansion through regional integration programs and to extend these possibilities to the rest of the world.

From the perspective of economic history, it is important to note the connections between Prebisch's thinking and that of other economists who were then beginning to consider the same problems. The concept of economic development was not much used before the 1940s.[10] It is true that, starting with the monumental *Inquiry into the Nature and Causes of the Wealth of Nations* by Adam Smith (1776), classical economists tried to identify the causes of economic growth and to analyze the processes of long-term change. It might be said that what Adam Smith termed "the causes of the wealth of nations" is what was later called "economic development." Nevertheless, after the publication in 1848 of John Stuart Mill's *Principles of Political Economy*, concern about economic development or growth entered a period of decline. The marginalist focus of neoclassical economists introduced a context of quantitative analysis and shifted interest to the more specific problems of allocating resources and the processes of trade. During the depression between the two world wars, the Keynesian view prevailed, centered on the analysis of short-term economic cycles, the potential threat of a secular trend toward economic stagnation in the advanced capitalist countries and possible remedies for it. It was only in the 1940s, as a result of the concern about creating a world order at the end of the war that would prevent a repetition of such conflicts, that the concept of development began to be utilized once again.

At first, most of the economists interested in these problems defined development in terms of increased per capita income in underdeveloped countries. Simon Kuznets linked the growth of per capita income to a series of structural changes that historically accompanied this process and to the social and institutional transfor-

Latin American ideas and their replication in development literature

---

[9] J. Hodara, op. cit., p. 22. See also E. Dosman and D. Pollock, op. cit.
[10] H.W. Arndt, "Economic Development: Semantic History," in *Economic Development and Cultural Change,* April 1981.

mations necessary to bring about such growth.[11] Of such transformations, industrialization stood out from the very beginning. Economists such as Paul Rosenstein-Rodan and Kurt Mandelbaum stressed its importance, pointing to the most underdeveloped countries of Eastern and Southeastern Europe.[12] It was assumed that economically depressed areas were negatively affected by their lack of industrial development, which kept a large percentage of their work force occupied in rural or urban activities with a very low level of productivity, and these countries were held up as an example of densely populated areas with a high percentage of hidden unemployment. It was also noted that weak demand and capital shortages were the main barriers to the creation of more productive employment. State intervention was necessary to overcome these barriers, both for the purpose of implementing redistributive measures to increase consumption and for promoting a process of forced savings aimed at increasing the rate of capital formation.

At the close of the Second World War, this concern shifted to what are now known as the developing countries. Except for Latin America, which led an independent life for more than a century but whose integration into the world economy was secondary to its special relationship with the United States, this group of countries was practically ignored. With the process of decolonization that began immediately after the Second World War with the independence or creation of Burma, Ceylon, the Philippines, India, Indonesia, Israel, Lebanon, Pakistan and Syria, followed later by many other countries, the problems of development began to move to center stage. Nevertheless, these countries tended at first to define themselves as producers of raw materials rather than economies embarking on a more complex process of development, and their problems tended to be viewed in terms of stabilizing the prices of commodities. At the Bretton Woods Conference and in a number of later meetings and resolutions, many Latin American countries such as Brazil, Colombia and Cuba signed initiatives aimed at minimizing fluctuations in the prices of commodities and promoting the regulation of the respective markets. The emphasis on the need for industrialization was due in large part to the work of the United Nations agencies, especially ECLA.

---

[11] S. Kuznets, "Quantitative Aspects of the Economic Growth of Nations," in *Economic Development and Cultural Change,* October 1956, and *Six Lectures on Economic Growth,* Glencoe, The Free Press, 1959.

[12] P. Rosenstein-Rodan, "Problems of Industrialization of Eastern and Southeastern Europe," in *Economic Journal,* Vol. 53, June-September 1943, and K. Mandelbaum, *Industrialization of Backward Areas,* Oxford, Basil Blackwell, 1947.

Basic concepts of the Prebisch Report

Nevertheless, the questioning of these strategies and of their results began well before the writing of the Prebisch Report. In some cases it took the form of theoretical disputes in the field of development economics, such as the quarrel between structuralists and monetarists in the late 1950s, and in other cases more pragmatic considerations were involved, related to certain exaggerations of these policies and their consequences. These questions are discussed in the following chapters, with special emphasis on the period when they were the most intense, but to understand the motivations and trends revealed by the Report, this fact must be taken into account. Some of the criticisms that began to be heard at this time included the limitations of import substitution, the excessive emphasis on this sector to the detriment of agriculture, the fact that industry did not create the expected employment nor the financing necessary for development, that a relatively depressed agricultural sector continued being the source of a considerable portion of this financing, and that industrialization created a growing demand for imported capital and intermediate and manufactured goods, thereby increasing the external vulnerability of the region due to the fact that in an import substitution process, the elasticity of demand for this type of goods is greater than one.

The first questioning of his original thinking

"The practical importance of Prebisch's formulation is clear in the sway it held over development policies in the 1950s and 1960s and even subsequently. Despite academic criticism addressed to the persuasiveness of the theoretical case he formulated for protectionism, industrialization, and planning—for those were the critical conclusions—and mounting statistical evidence that the terms of trade had not shown a deterioration trend, import substitution dominated. It did so not merely because of the persuasiveness of Prebisch's ideas, but also because of the conditions then prevailing. In the 1950s the terms of trade eroded for many countries from cyclical Korean War highs and discouraged investment in the primary sector because industrialization in many Latin American countries had already reached levels at which national producers represented a significant political voice; increased direct foreign investment made transmission of technology more effective than it had been earlier, and also compensated for increasing deficits on trade account; and national autonomy and increasing state participation were popular political values.

"As we have all come to appreciate, and Prebisch among the first, import substitution was not an unmixed blessing. It was a second-best policy imposed to tax agriculture and reallocate resources toward industry that was eventually brought down by the very circumstance it was to avert: a shortage of foreign exchange. Import substitution's bias against exports and its own voracious appetite for imports of intermediate and capital goods created a fundamental disequilibrium. So, too, expanded state activity without concomitant revenues tended to provoke larger deficits and inflationary pressures; when real resource transfer from agriculture to industry became progressively more difficult because of a weaker balance of payments, subsidies to industry were financed by central banks. Finally, the hopes for massive absorption of labor in industry and a more equitable income distribution were dealt a blow by evidence of widening disparities and privileged, organized urban workers."[13]

The lessons of reality and the creation of UNCTAD

Prebisch was always the first to compare his ideas with reality, to criticize them and to adjust them to new circumstances. In accepting the responsibility to organize UNCTAD fifteen years after developing his first proposals, he clearly indicated the limits that import substition was approaching. "Industrialization is encountering growing difficulties in the countries where it is most advanced, difficulties caused by the narrowness of domestic markets and also by this peculiar fact: the more imports are replaced, the more other imports expand as primary income increases, due to the greater demand for capital goods and, consequently, the effects of more income. For some years now this pressure has been augmented by the adverse effects of the deterioration of the terms of trade, which have impaired the effectiveness of the inflows of international financial resources." And he concluded, in another part of this same analysis: "The growth of the capacity to import is quite different from satisfying the demand for imports created by economic development."

Although Prebisch had the opportunity to put his ideas to the test on a worldwide scale through UNCTAD, this experience intensified his self-criticism. International cooperation, he said in New Delhi, will be largely wasted unless the industrialized countries realize that the primary responsibility must be exercised within their borders. "This policy of internal development makes it absolutely necessary for the developing countries to embark with determination upon a series of changes in their structures and attitudes, if they have not already done so. And this also requires adhering to the discipline

---

[13] A. Fishlow, "Comment," Meier and Seers, op. cit., pp. 193-194.

of a development plan, promoting reciprocal trade through regional and subregional integration groups, and supporting interregional measures for the expansion of trade."[14]

The Prebisch Report is based on the principal ideas of Latin American thinking on development summarized above, takes into account the aforementioned limitations and criticisms, and looks to the future. This triple outlook is the basis of the fundamental ideas of the Report. It also forms the basis of the theses concerning the dynamic lack of growth in Latin America: the persistence of an inadequate employment structure, the waste of human potential and the spurious absorption of the work force after several decades of policies aimed at industrial promotion; that productivity and employment do not increase concomitantly but rather in a disjointed and sometimes contradictory manner, and that they do not respond in a parallel fashion to the rate of economic growth;[15] the need to promote social integration and expansion of the domestic market through effective distributive policies; to understand and properly assimilate scientific and technological advances, their benefits and their contradictions; and the necessity of decisively accelerating capital formation in order to respond to these needs, and that of seeking a much higher level of international cooperation on both the financial and the commercial levels. According to the Prebisch Report, the conversion of these theses into policies and then into results is the key to overcoming the limitations of the outward-oriented development stage described above, as well as the easiest alternative with populist and redistributive interest for adopting a new "discipline of development" aimed at the assimilation and harmonization of all these theories.

The Report's basic premise: the growing inadequacy of Latin American development

"To go from a relatively slow pace of development and few social objectives to a pace that corrects the growing inadequacy of the economy together with a pronounced social orientation requires considerable effort in the areas of converting structures and practicing true developmental discipline, especially in the formation of capital and the promotion of foreign trade. This is unavoidable. If powerful obstacles to the practice of a conscientious discipline arise, development will become imperative one way or another, because frustration, whether it is the frustration of maintaining the status quo

The discipline of development

---

[14] R. Prebisch, *Nueva política comercial para el desarrollo,* Mexico, Fondo de Cultura Económica, 1964, pages 20 and 30.

[15] This hypothesis contradicted the basic tenets of Keynesian economic theory and was quantitatively demonstrated only recently.

or of populism, is not an alternative. The advantage of this populist movement has been that great social evils have been exposed and the people have been encouraged in their aspirations toward social integration. Nevertheless, in the absence of strong convictions and a well-articulated system of ideas, populism plays endlessly upon the emotions and raises charismatic personalities to high positions. This avoids the difficult problems and substitutes immediate redistribution for the real transformations and thorough solutions that development requires. Populism cannot therefore be considered an alternative to the discipline of development....A great internal effort, an imperative, unavoidable effort, is necessary. Is success possible without the adoption of compulsory measures?"[16] This last question anticipates the course taken by the governments of various countries of the region in the 1970s.

The Report emphasized many of the premises, limitations and options of the prevailing ideas on Latin American development in light of the given circumstances, and did so not only on the economic but also the political plane, an interrelationship that would be stressed in the subsequent evolution of Prebisch's thinking.

Prebisch's intellectual legacy

Since Raúl Prebisch wrote his report—ten years after the founding of the Inter-American Development Bank—the world has changed dramatically and so has Latin America. In the next chapter I will examine the evolution and obsolescence of the region's postwar development model. Farther on, I will analyze the crisis the region subsequently experienced, the discussion of various models sparked by the crisis and the consensus that seems to be emerging for ending the crisis. However, since history is by definition a mixture of continuities and changes, I believe it essential to describe what Latin America was like when Prebisch was developing his seminal ideas and when he wrote his Report.[17] Prebisch's ideas were discussed and

---

[16] R. Prebisch, *Transformación y desarrollo: la gran tarea de América Latina*, Mexico, Fondo de Cultura Económica, 1970, p. 17.

[17] For a more detailed description of this period see the book *Una década de lucha por América Latina,* coordinated by A. Calvo and L. Tomassini to commemorate the tenth anniversary of the founding of the IDB, published in 1970 in Mexico by the Fondo de Cultura Económica.

were also changed many times as a result of his open mind and his attention to new events and trends. It has been said that over time Prebisch presented "multiple images," and the explanation has been given that each of these was the reflection that the circumstances of each period created in his mind, thus there is a clearly discernible thread through all of them.[18]

There can be no doubt that the life and work of Raúl Prebisch are a remarkable contribution to understanding the specific problems of Latin America and development theory in general. "To place Raúl Prebisch among a *large* field of 'pioneers' or 'fathers' of development economics is to lose perspective. For those of us who grew up through the 1950s, it is immediately apparent that Prebisch (along with Paul Rosenstein-Rodan, Ragnar Nurkse, and W.A. Lewis, to mention several of the important figures that influenced my generation) belongs to a most distinguished *small* group of pioneers—if 'pioneers' refers to Columbus rather than the Mayflower immigrants."[19] But the forcefulness and permanence of Prebisch's ideas are due not so much to his ability to describe the economic development problems of Latin America and to propose solutions in each stage, for this would mean that his thinking changed along with circumstances, but rather to the fact that he bequeathed to us a series of analytical methods and categories, many of which are still valid today.

The most important contribution: analytical methods and strategies

Of these, I would first mention his fierce intellectual autonomy. Prebisch begins the essay in which he traces the evolution of his economic thinking by declaring: "When I started my life as a young economist and professor during the 1920s, I was a firm believer in neoclassical theories. However, the first great crisis of capitalism—the world Depression—prompted in me serious doubts regarding these beliefs. It was the beginning of a long period of heresies, as I tried to explore new views on development matters."[20] After that, Raúl Prebisch never belonged to any school of thought and, contrary to popular belief, he never attempted to create any either. This explains his intellectual peregrination through a wide variety of subjects, creating new ideas and institutions at every stage: the center-periphery relationship, industrialization, planning and international trade or the development of peripheral capitalism. Thus, in his conversations, Raúl Prebisch especially enjoyed people who offered criticisms or who saw things from a new perspective, in

Intellectual autonomy

---

[18] See the document by E. Dosman and D. Pollock cited previously.

[19] J. N. Bhagwati, "Comment," in Meier and Seers, op. cit., p. 197.

[20] In Meier and Seers, op. cit., p. 175.

21

which case he would often exclaim: "You must develop that idea further!" This was the genesis of many articles published by the Journal of the ECLA when he headed it. The failure or inadequacy of traditional economic models and the confusion of ideas created by the crisis make such intellectual autonomy the first prerequisite of the search for solutions.

Prebisch's critical spirit

A second quality we must bring to economic analysis is the ability to criticize, which is always evident in Prebisch's thinking. Raúl Prebisch was able to participate in the development policies of a commodity exporting country such as Argentina in the thirties and, at the same time, to criticize those policies; to develop the center-periphery system of analysis and, later, to question it; to advocate import substitution in one stage and subsequently to criticize its excesses; to propose a program to stabilize the prices of commodities and then to note its meager results; and to recognize the successes of peripheral capitalism without ceasing to question the nature of the process. It is interesting to note that he always criticized many of his own ideas and that some of his followers later founded schools of thought on these same ideas.

Another extraordinary virtue of Prebisch's thinking in each of its various stages is his ability to pay equal attention to the ideas, the policies and the institutions necessary to implement them. Prebisch not only reflected his concern for these three aspects in all his writings, he demonstrated them throughout his life, inspiring policies and creating institutions.

Relationship between ideas and policies

Few economists have had the opportunity that Prebisch had throughout his life to experience so many crises and emergency situations: the Great Depression of the 1930s, the Second World War and the ensuing reconstruction, the isolation of Latin America during this period, the oil crises, the subsequent series of recessions in the industrialized economies, the debt explosion in Latin America and the consequences of the adjustment policies. It could be said that Prebisch's thinking developed between one emergency and the next. Nevertheless, few thinkers and economists have been able to reconcile so well as he did in all stages of his work, the short, the medium and the long term.

Not many analysts of the development process, especially since economic thinking began to focus on these subjects, have emphasized as strongly as Prebisch did the importance of the foreign market to the economic growth of the developing countries and the interaction that always exists between the external world and their internal economic development. To be more specific, I would say that although most of the founders of development theory ascribed great importance to the external factors in this process, few included so wide a range of variables as Prebisch did—and the schools inspired by his thinking—and few so clearly perceived the extent of the interaction between the external and the internal planes. This vision was not incorporated in the economic thinking of the industrialized countries until much later, when they began to analyze the phenomena of transnationalization and interdependence.

Contrary to popular belief, at a time when the liberal policies made possible by the emergence of modern industrial states were still not coordinated with the Keynesian policies introduced in response to the crisis, Prebisch always expressed very strong concern about the interaction that should exist between the State and the market, a concern that constitutes another of the many analytical categories we have inherited from him.

The emphasis on the external context

Another of the dichotomies overcome in Prebisch's thinking concerns growth and equity. During Prebisch's adult life, political affiliations and conflicts in Latin America were largely centered on these two opposites. Prebisch's thinking always ascribed importance to both objectives and inevitably sought ways of reconciling them.

Concern about equity

One of his most visionary contributions, which is still not fully appreciated, is the priority Prebisch assigned to the incorporation of technical progress as the keystone of development. It is impossible to know with any certainty today whether he was aware, more than 40 years ago when he advanced this theory, of the importance it would have in the next stage of long-term world economic development, i.e., our own era, in which there is no doubt that development depends essentially on technological innovation and knowledge. Moreover, as in the case of the other analytical categories mentioned above, this is true regardless of what the leading sectors of the economy are at any given moment in its historical evolution.[21]

The role of technological innovation

In this same connection, we are aware today that Prebisch was one of the thinkers who included in his analysis a larger number of noneconomic variables and who encouraged his followers to do the same, starting with the appointment of the prominent Spanish sociologist, José Medina Echavarría, to ECLA thirty years ago.

Use of non-economic variables

---

[21] One of the intellectuals who best understood and did the most to update this perception of Prebisch was Fernando Fajnzylber, who died prematurely as these lines were being written. See *La industrialización trunca de América Latina,* Mexico, Nueva Imagen, 1980, and *Industrialización en América Latina: de la caja negra al casillero vacío*, ECLA 1990, as well as Fajnzylber's important contributions to the recent thinking of the ECLA.

Clearly, the complex, multidisciplinary nature of the problems of development in today's world requires this focus.

Finally, and reading into the text somewhat of Prebisch, there is a concept in his Report that evokes, although not explicitly, a concept that was ultimately forgotten and which is now extremely relevant: the idea that there must be a "development discipline," not applicable, obviously, to the ideas or institutions that are part of this process, but to the agents or participants therein.

At this stage of world and Latin American economic development, and owing to the erosion of confidence in the State's ability to unilaterally solve the numerous problems posed by modern society, it is increasingly clear that the efforts of the State, society and the market must be joined in a productive alliance involving the action of many social and economic agents, whose proliferation is one of the characteristics of contemporary society. The discipline this harmonization requires is assuredly the ethical and social force Raúl Prebisch was thinking of when he introduced the concept in the Report published over 20 years ago.

Evolution and crisis of the economies of Latin America

The obsolescence of the postwar development model

In 1950, most of the countries of Latin America implemented an import substitution strategy. It has already been noted that this strategy seemed appropriate, especially in the beginning, given the conditions created by the Great Depression of the 1930s and the Second World War, which were followed by the boom caused by the Korean War. During these years the international economy seemed little able to provide the stimulus for Latin American growth, while the United States, as it demonstrated with the Marshall Plan, assigned its highest priorities to the reconstruction of Europe and the Cold War.

An unconventional view of development

Retrospective analysis reveals the influence exerted in this process by a group of economists who met at ECLA under the leadership of Dr. Raúl Prebisch, whose influence at the time in both the theory and practice of Latin American development was very great. Of course, as already mentioned, these ideas were largely a systematization of the economic experience of the Latin American governments during this period. In any case, this view differed from the orthodox view of economic growth in several ways: first, from the macroeconomic viewpoint, because of its perception of the inadequate role the international markets played in the development of the Latin American countries, together with the emphasis placed by conventional development theory on domestic savings as a preponderant factor in capital formation, which was replaced by concern about the restrictions on flows of foreign resources resulting, for the most part, from the trend toward deterioration of the terms of trade of the countries of the region. This led directly to the recommendation to replace imports through the domestic production of a growing range of products that were previously imported, and to save the little foreign exchange available to buy the equipment and basic inputs needed for development.

Second, from a more microeconomic perspective, the Latin American view stressed the existence of distortions and inconsistencies that hindered the normal operation of the markets and the proper functioning of the price systems, including the concentration of land ownership, incipient and poorly integrated industrial development and, in general, the structural disparateness of Latin America's productive systems. All of these factors made it impossible at this stage to promote development on a fully competitive basis.

These two elements necessitated extensive, well-planned State intervention in the economy: the belief was that development should be the result of deliberate policies and not the spontaneous product of unfettered competition; these policies should be oriented toward objectives selected through a careful planning process; and the State, in addition to formulating these plans and policies, should intervene in a certain number of specific sectors to eliminate or reduce the above-mentioned restrictions or inconsistencies and to promote industrial activities crucial to the growth of production.

The results of the prevailing model

The results of the development efforts of the Latin American countries in the following thirty years were truly impressive. Latin America as a whole experienced considerable growth during this period. The region's gross domestic product (GDP) grew at a rate above 5.5 percent per annum. This rate surpassed the growth achieved in not only other developing regions of the world but also in most of the industrialized countries, the only exceptions being the oil-producing countries, the socialist countries and Japan. Consequently, regional production quadrupled during this period and industrial production and foreign trade expanded at even faster rates, especially in the latter sector, in the second half of the period.

Despite the adverse effects of a high demographic growth rate, the average per capita product in Latin America increased at a rate of roughly 3 percent per annum, reaching a level greater than $1,300 at current prices until 1980, which placed the region in the middle of the international ranking, representing what became known as an intermediate level of economic development. Although this growth was inferior to that of most of the industrialized countries, except the United States, it compared favorably with the goal of 2 per cent per annum proposed by the Alliance for Progress, the region's most important program of external cooperation for development throughout this period.

This growth rate was accompanied by a comparatively intense process of investment and productive and technological transformation in the Latin American economies. The region's industrial capacity was diversified considerably, making it possible for domestic production to satisfy nearly all of the demand for consumer goods and a substantial portion of the intermediate and capital goods, as well as to promote the expanding diversification of Latin American exports, with manufactures representing an ever increasing share. Agriculture was also being gradually transformed through the introduction of modern production techniques, advances in productive organization and product marketing, and greater market integration. The infrastructure was also significantly enlarged, particularly in the fields of energy, transportation and communications. Thus, toward the end of the period, the various national economies had increased their level of integration and sectoral interdependence, which was later to prove a very important factor in their modernization efforts.

The diversity of national experiences

The pace and characteristics of the economic development of the Latin American countries in this period were not uniform. Differences, and even contrasts, were noted in the specific growth of the different countries. These are explained by the differences in the size and structure of their national economies, their natural resources, their individual ways of entering the world economy and their ability to react to changes in the international markets. National policies strongly influenced each country's economic performance. The most impressive results were obtained by Brazil, which increased its share of the regional product from 22 percent to more than 34 percent, and Mexico, whose success was also remarkable. At the other extreme, in certain countries such as those of the Southern Cone, which had enjoyed a promising level of development before the war, and in others such as the Central American countries, economic growth slowed dramatically.

The development process of the Latin American countries was not consistent during this period either. In the first stage, between 1950 and 1965, the rate of economic growth was substantial, climbing to more than 5 percent per annum, but exports grew slowly and the terms of trade deteriorated, especially after the Korean War; imports grew at a pace that was less than half the rate of increase in the gross domestic product, which began to fall during this period, while the ability to borrow abroad and the availability of financing were extremely low. The growth of external demand was also an important factor in the economic performance of the Latin American countries. During this period, exports grew at a much lower rate than the increase in the domestic product, while the terms of trade deteriorated. The purchasing power of the exports of the Latin American countries as a whole increased during this period at an annual average rate of only 2 percent, while the gross domestic product grew at a rate of 5.2 percent per annum. These trends refer

Differences in rates and in time: the 1950-1965 period

basically to the large and medium-sized countries, while small countries such as those in Central America managed to increase the purchasing power of their exports. An exception was Brazil, where the purchasing power of exports remained virtually unchanged despite the fact that the country's domestic product increased an average of 6 percent per annum.

The 1965-1975 period

The second stage, between 1965 and the mid-1970s, was distinctly different from the first: the average annual rate of increase in the gross domestic product was 6.7 percent in the 1965-1974 period, with the performance of the oil-exporting countries having a particular impact in the last two years, as external conditions tended to improve, quickening the growth rate of the industrialized countries and intensifying external demand, which, at the end of this stage, brought about a positive change in the terms of trade. These stimuli were accompanied by gradual changes in the external economic policies of the Latin American countries, which were oriented toward increased liberalization of their foreign trade and the promotion of exports, the purchasing power of which began to increase faster than the gross domestic product (6.7 percent as compared with 6.3 percent, respectively).

Since the availability of foreign credit increased at the same time, the potential to import also expanded, the most remarkable case perhaps being Brazil, where the import-domestic product ratio climbed from 4.8 percent in 1964-1966 to 8.3 percent in 1971-1973. Generally, in most of the Latin American countries, the downward trend in import ratios observed in the preceding period was halted, and the capacity to import increased significantly. Between 1965 and 1974, the domestic product of the non-oil-exporting countries, for the region as a whole, grew at an annual rate of 7.7 percent, while their merchandise imports increased at a rate of 9.6 percent per annum. The situation was even more positive in the oil-exporting countries.

The latter half of the 1970s is characterized by quite different situations and trends in the various countries, due to the external imbalances of the seventies, their individual situations with respect to external indebtedness, their productive capacity and export potential, the policies implemented to deal with the repercussions of the increase in oil prices, the slow and uneven recovery of the growth rate of the industrialized countries following the 1974-1975 recession, and the balance of payments difficulties caused essentially by the external debt problem, which is discussed in the following section.

One of the most striking results of the strategies followed by the Latin American countries in the postwar era is the level of institutional development attained by the region. Early in the period, central banks were relatively new and not all countries had them, and very few had created national development banks such as *Nacional Financiera* in Mexico and *Corporación de Fomento de la Producción* in Chile. During this period, almost all of the countries created national planning systems, development financing institutions, national savings and loan systems, agricultural development or agrarian reform institutions, efficiently organized public services that made it possible to improve the infrastructure in the field of transportation and communications, national energy companies, modern higher education institutions, national science and technology systems, and other agencies that contributed to an accelerated modernization process. In general, this resulted in a substantial improvement in the process of mobilizing domestic resources, providing social services, constructing and maintaining the physical infrastructure, improving the tax systems, and developing the educational, scientific and technological systems. This robust institutional growth was linked, on the one hand, to the role the State played in the implementation of this development strategy, while, on the other, it was probably the most important of the factors that helped to convert many Latin American countries into modern nations.

Postwar institutional development

However, in the early seventies, when Dr. Prebisch's Report criticized the dynamic lack of Latin American growth, the import substitution strategy had revealed serious internal shortcomings that evoked the criticisms mentioned above.

Onset of the crisis: three basic imbalances

The substitution of imports led to an essentially disproportionate development process that promptly encountered three limitations, which gradually became apparent: the erosion of the trade balance, increased sectoral imbalances and the deterioration of public sector accounts.

Protectionism led to overvalued exchange rates and, consequently, to a form of export tax. The inadequate growth of exports was a very serious obstacle to the industrialization process, which required growing inputs of capital and intermediate goods. As trade deficits mounted, these inputs began to depend more on foreign investment and foreign aid. Paradoxically, the so-called outward-oriented growth strategy, based on promoting the countries' own productive capacity, led to increasing dependence on countries outside the region.

Concurrently, and as a counterpart of the vigorous process of institutional development described above, a burgeoning, inefficient bureaucracy began to appear, whose job was to impose a series of frequently contradictory regulations aimed at monitoring the level of protectionism and the management of the exchange rates. The first criticism leveled against the postwar economic strategy, therefore, was its failure to promote exports.[22]

From a sectoral perspective, the import substitution policy provided excessive protection of industry to the detriment of agriculture, which had three negative consequences. First, the prices of agricultural products were kept artificially low, which benefited urban incomes at the expense of the rural population. Second, since industry was more capital-intensive than agriculture, it only absorbed a small percentage of the increase in the work force. The rest of these workers were forced to take low-productivity jobs in agriculture, in marginal occupations and in urban areas, or they exerted pressure on the public sector to find them work. Third, in planning, it was determined that the setting of physical objectives was more important than the cost-benefit analysis in the financing of investment projects, while the high price of foreign exchange made it difficult to justify the projects.

The third imbalance associated with this strategy appeared in the tax system. As foreign receipts from raw material exports declined and income from exports of manufactures failed to materialize, subsidies for the industrial sector had to come from taxes. At the same time, the State's responsibilities had increased, which put additional pressure on government budgets. The monetization of fiscal deficits, a practice dating from the 19th century, unleashed the chronic inflationary pressures that have troubled Latin America for so many years.

The model begins to prove inadequate

At the start of the sixties, as a result of the poor performance of Latin American exports and the expansionist macroeconomic policies followed by the countries of the region, many countries experienced recurring deficits in their balance of payments and escalating inflationary processes. Among these were Argentina, Bolivia, Brazil, Colombia, Chile and Uruguay. The measures recommended in these circumstances by the International Monetary Fund, aimed at controlling expenditures and adjusting and unifying exchange rates, were contradictory to the policies followed until then by the countries of the region. The aim of these policies with regard to inflationary pressures was to deepen the industrialization process,

---

[22] Among these critics were I. Little, T. Scitovsky, and M. Scott, *Industry and Trade in Some Developing Countries: A Comparative Essay*, New York, Oxford University Press, 1970; B. Balassa, et al., *The Structure of Protection in Developed Countries*, Baltimore, Johns Hopkins University Press, 1971; and J. Bhagwati, *Anatomy and Consequences of Trade Control Regimes,* Cambridge, Mass., National Bureau of Economic Research, 1978.

attribute inflation to supply side restrictions and expand the markets in which this process operated through the promotion of regional integration programs.

By then, both Raúl Prebisch and ECLA were deeply concerned about the inadequacies of the industrialization and import substitution policies and began to express the necessity of moving in a new direction. In 1959 Dr. Prebisch wrote: "Trade between the Latin-American countries forms only 10 percent of their total foreign trade, and industrial exports are relatively very small by contrast with countries such as Italy, Japan, and others with similar income levels. All this has resulted in the splitting of the industrialization process into as many watertight compartments as there are countries, without the advantages of specialization and the economies of scale."[23] These ideas gave birth to the Latin American Free Trade Association (LAFTA) and the Andean Pact. But, in the long run, import substitution at the regional level proved to be much more difficult than at the national level. With the perspective provided by time, it can now be conjectured that the confidence placed in the expansion of markets through regional integration programs drew attention away from the need to reduce or to simplify the protection afforded the industrialization process.

In the mid-seventies problems had begun to multiply, which slowed the economic growth of the Latin American countries. The effects of the rise in oil prices and the international recession on the Latin American economies, which they tried to alleviate through foreign borrowing, taking advantage of the unusual conditions then prevailing in the international financial markets, were all the more acute because of the added burden of their own problems. This conclusion is based on the fact that the impact of the world economic crisis on Latin America was greater than it was on any other region of the developing world, except Africa.

Latin American industrialization failed to discover the road to effective international competition—unlike the countries of Southeast Asia, which did so subsequently in a much more dynamic manner—and, consequently, the foreign resources necessary to sustain and ultimately expand it were not forthcoming. The bias against agriculture, which ought to have provided some of these resources,

Loss of international competitiveness

---

[23] R. Prebisch, "Commercial Policy in the Underdeveloped Countries," in *American Economic Review,* May 1959. See also R. Prebisch, *Nueva política comercial para el desarrollo,* Mexico, Fondo de Cultura Económica, 1964, and A. Hirschman, *Latin American Issues: Essays and Comments,* New York, Twentieth Century Fund, 1961.

accentuated the impact of the terms of trade trend deterioration on raw material export earnings. Industrial development also failed to generate the capacity to absorb the redundant rural work force to the extent originally anticipated. It permitted the persistence or worsening of the social problems that these countries had traditionally faced.

Runaway inflation

External account imbalances and fiscal deficits, which were closely associated with the prevailing development pattern, made these problems even worse by adding "inflationary tax" effects. The shock felt by the Latin American countries in the wake of the world economic crisis makes it difficult to determine to what extent the decision to resort to foreign indebtedness resulted from this latter cause or was prompted by an insufficient response capability on the part of the Latin American economies.

The above comments contrast with the fact that throughout this century, Latin America was the world's fastest growing region, with an average annual rate of 13.8 percent between 1900 and 1987, as compared with a rate of 2.9 percent for the countries that subsequently became part of the OECD, 3.2 percent for the Asian countries and 3.3 percent for the Soviet Union (according to Professor Angus Maddison's statistics).[24] They are also corroborated by the recent extraordinary growth of the Southeast Asian economies, which implemented export-oriented development policies.

Loss of positions in the international markets

One indication of the above is that when the payments crisis erupted in 1982, Latin America's external debt was approximately three times the value of its exports, while the indebtedness of South Korea, which had also grown considerably in recent years, represented only about a third of its exports. Paradoxically, the extraordinary bonanza in the international financial markets, recovered after almost fifty years, went a long way toward fulfilling the prophecy implicit in the external pessimism that characterized Latin American economic thinking until this time. It is also paradoxical to conjecture, as will be seen later, that the external crisis, which had more serious consequences for Latin America during these same fifty years, may have helped to destroy this pessimism and to force the countries of the region to modernize their economic systems, open their economies to international trade and seek to expand exports.

At this time, considerable pessimism concerning the elasticity of Latin American exports with respect to foreign demand was justifiable, not only because of their terms of trade trend deterioration but also because there was reason to expect that greater dynamism in

---

[24] See *The World Economy in the Twentieth Century,* OECD, Paris, 1989.

Latin American economic growth would eventually conflict with the growing protectionist trends in the centers. Interestingly, almost all of the development theories of the period shared this pessimism.

Ragnar Nurkse, in the lectures collected in *Patterns of Trade and Development* (Stockholm, 1959), obviously influenced by events in the period following the depression, predicted that foreign trade would cease to be the "engine of growth" of the developing countries and proposed an inward-oriented development strategy. This involved an import substitution process, since the instability of its terms of trade would force Latin America to rely on domestic demand. Nurkse did not specify to what extent this strategy meant going beyond the market economy, since he believed in the possibility of establishing an optimal level of protectionism correctly reflecting the elasticity of the primary exports of the developing countries with respect to external demand.

Nevertheless, Professor Paul Rosenstein-Rodan had earlier argued (in *Problems of the Industrialization of Eastern and South Eastern Europe*, 1943) that underdeveloped countries faced a situation of imbalance characterized by the lack of incentives to invest in one sector because of the lack of investments in others, together with the fact that the extreme instability of their terms of trade made access to foreign markets difficult, all of which justified a high degree of pessimism concerning the role of demand and made State planning a necessity. The call for planning had strong precedents in the policies of the New Deal in the United States and in the war effort, as well as the development models of the Soviet Union and India, during the postwar era in the latter case.

Early theoretical criticisms of the model

It is important to remember that as early as the 1950s, in a series of lectures given in Rio de Janeiro, Professor Jacob Viner had rejected arguments favoring the protection of industries competing with imported goods and had recommended an end to the discrimination against exports, together with improved functioning of the price system.[25] Another critic of the structuralist view of development at

---

[25] J. Viner, *International Trade and Economic Development*, Oxford, Clarendon Press, Clarendon, 1953. It is interesting to see how C. Furtado recalls his argument in *La fantasía organizada*, Buenos Aires, EUDEBA, 1985.

the time was the Brazilian economist Roberto Campos, who questioned the bias that favored industry over agriculture, the distrust of private initiative and the emphasis on the public sector, and the tendency to think that inflation could contribute to capital formation in developing countries.[26]

New analytical instruments in trade policy

At that time, new analytical instruments were being developed, especially in the area of trade policy. Thus, for example, the concept of effective protection, which had begun to be formulated in the 1950s, became established and gained currency as a result of an influential document of Professor W. M. Corden published in 1966.[27] This concept provided an understanding of the impact of the tariff structure on the value added of products, as well as the economic effects of other types of distortions. It also made it possible to distinguish between measures aimed at the protection of industry and those intended to promote exports. The result of all this was a more accurate evaluation of the trade regulations of the developing countries. It is interesting to note that in 1964, Santiago Macario of ECLA had employed the concept of effective protection to critically analyze the process of industrialization in Latin America.[28]

Necessity of placing criticism in the historical context

To place these criticisms in the proper historical context it is necessary to recall once more that they were made 30 or 40 years after the import substitution process in Latin America had begun as a pragmatic response to the negative consequences of the depression of the 1930s. The Great Depression caused a dramatic fall in the prices and volumes of Latin American exports. This made it extremely difficult to procure the imports the region needed and it created incentives to establish industries to replace such products. The Second World War reinforced this trend since the war effort of the industrialized countries necessitated a reorientation of their industrial output toward strategic objectives and a cutback in their exports of manufactures to Latin America. The gradual increase in tariff protection and the creation of industrial credit incentives were additional measures to stimulate this process. The underestimation of the market's ability to overcome the crisis and the specific bias

---

[26] R. Campos, "To the Use of Inflation in Latin America," in A. Hirschman, op. cit.

[27] W. M. Corden, "The Structure of a Tariff System and the Effective Protective Rates," in *Journal of Political Economy,* August 1966.

[28] For other external criticisms of the structuralist school see I. Little, T. Scitovsky and M. Scott, *Industry and Trade in Some Developing Countries: A Comparative Study,* New York, Oxford University Press, 1970; B. Balassa et al., op. cit.

that this distrust created in Latin America in the form of extreme external pessimism also reflected a global trend toward Keynesianism, which favored an active market, not to replace the market but rather to support it by allowing an anti-cyclical policy to develop. Finally, the inability to import created by the depression, the war and the global ascendancy of Keynesianism were the specific short-term factors that allowed Prebisch to formulate his perception of a secular trend toward deterioration of the terms of trade of countries that exported raw materials and, therefore, the necessity of promoting planned industrialization processes as the only way to escape this trend in the long term. This theory has been one of the most controversial of all of Prebisch's ideas. But the economic thinking and development strategies of the Latin American countries in the postwar era can only be understood within the context of this historic experience.

Just as the first steps toward import substitution in Latin America were a practical response to adverse conditions, so were the initial efforts of liberalization and deregulation basically experimental and not always as persistent as they should have been. Toward the middle of the 1960s, Brazil undertook a series of reforms aimed at improving the functioning of its markets and the performance of its export activities, including more realistic exchange rates, the elimination of export duties, the introduction of tax and credit incentives for these activities, reduction of the fiscal deficit, the curbing of inflation, development of the capital markets and some control over real wages. The results of this policy were remarkable. Between 1968 and 1973 the Brazilian economy grew at an average annual rate of 11 percent, and between 1973 and 1977 at an annual rate of 7.7 percent, while exports expanded an average of 23 percent per year between 1968 and 1977. In 1967 Colombia implemented similar policies, aimed at eliminating export barriers and adopting a more realistic exchange rate policy, with the result that the growth of its exports, which had been 2.7 percent per annum between 1961 and 1967, increased to 19.1 percent between 1968 and 1977. Argentina, Chile, Mexico, Uruguay and other countries tried similar policies at various times during this period.

In the 1970s these early trade liberalization and monetary stabilization efforts were followed by certain economic reforms undertaken more or less by the same countries that had championed such experiments. Import substitution policies came under heavier attack where they had been followed more intensively and for longer periods of time, and where macroeconomic problems were the most severe, as in the countries of the Southern Cone of Latin America.

The beginning of a reaction in economic policy: the export effort

After the first jump in oil prices, the balance of payments problems of these countries worsened.

Due to a number of factors, which certainly included mounting economic problems, military governments sooner or later seized power in almost all of these countries and joined forces with liberal economic teams that instituted economic reforms aimed not only at curbing inflation and opening the economies but also reducing the State's role and intensifying the utilization of markets in an attempt to speed up the integration of these countries in the international economy. These reforms began in Chile and Uruguay in 1974 and in Argentina in 1976.

Stabilization efforts

At first, the countries tried to base their anti-inflationary policies on a sharp reduction in their fiscal deficits and money supplies through drastic spending cuts and tax reforms. The limitations of policies aimed at reducing spending also led to efforts to modify it by changing the relative prices of imported goods as well as between importable and exportable goods. These changes were made through various combinations of measures, including sizable real devaluations, fewer import barriers, lower export duties and subsidies for nontraditional exports.

Finally, because of the persistence of inflationary processes, the exchange rate began to be used as the principal stabilizing tool, frequently through programmed devaluations.

Microeconomic discipline

The efforts in these countries to control inflation and balance external accounts were accompanied by a series of microeconomic measures. In all of them, various forms of government intervention or intermediation were eliminated, price controls were abolished, interest rates were decontrolled, labor markets were partially deregulated, restrictions on foreign trade were relaxed and the entry of foreign capital was made easier. The pace and sequence of these reforms varied from country to country, except for the deregulation of financial markets, which occurred quickly in all of them. The latter included eliminating interest rate ceilings and lowering the restrictions on financial agents. Severity in this regard had become very important after years in which credit had been relegated to the margins of the price system and in which very low or simply negative interest rates prevailed. These reforms produced some positive results, but not all of them lasted. The persistence of fiscal deficits in some countries, the second hike in oil prices in the late 1980s and continued access to international credit on unusually favorable terms, which was used both to alleviate fiscal problems and to combat inflation through exchange lag, in many cases deflected the aim of these measures. These policies, moreover, were never consistently followed in all of the countries, at least not until the second increase in oil prices and the debt payment crisis, after which the implementation of these measures began to be generalized. An outstanding example of coherent and efficient administration throughout the period in question is Colombia, which demonstrated admirable consistency and persistence in its economic policies.

Just as the criticism of import substitution and the implementation of economic reforms began well before the financial crisis of the 1980s, so did the debate about the role of the State. The basic principles of the development strategies followed by the Latin American countries in the postwar era revealed a conspicuous lack of confidence in market forces to deal with the problems of underdevelopment and, above all, to correct the distortions that prevented their resolution, resulting in a high degree of State intervention. The lack of foreign resources, which, according to the prevailing view, was the principal barrier to development and seemed inherent in the inward-oriented growth strategy, had been addressed through the imposition of additional taxes or stricter administrative controls on imports and capital movements. The effort to correct the persistent trend toward increased public spending and the ensuing chronic inflationary trends consisted of controlling prices, which, although it temporarily helped to curb inflation, was unfortunately even more effective in slowing production. To stimulate production, it was necessary to resort to tax exemptions or credit subsidies. Thus, the interplay of market forces was gradually being replaced by discretionary measures taken by the State.

At the same time, the private sector, instead of showing initiative, taking risks and contributing to economic growth, became accustomed to petitioning the government for tariff protections, tax exemptions, preferential credits and fixed prices. This is why, in the 1960s, various countries started questioning the excessive and costly interference of the State in economic activities and began to express support for the reduction of public spending, the elimination of fiscal deficits, the slowing of excessive growth of taxes, the privatization of certain productive activities controlled by the public sector, and the liberalization of prices and foreign trade, especially through the establishment of low, uniform tariffs and what today would be called a certain degree of deregulation of the labor and capital markets.

These concerns were validated by the fact that in the 1970s, the State had clearly failed to manage three policy areas that were traditionally its responsibility: macroeconomics, taxation and distribution. In the first instance, repeated and cumulative excesses paved the way for inflation above three digits in the 1980s, the accrual of disproportionate external deficits and high levels of unemployment. The persistent inability of many countries of the region to implement modern, equitable and easily-understood tax systems was another reason for questioning the State's role: it was said that in those years the Latin American governments spent like developed countries and collected taxes like feudal nations.[29] Finally, compared to the magnitude of the problems, the advances in the redistribution of income and the fight against poverty were generally insignificant, although the absolute income of the poorest groups tended to improve during this period. Such was not the case with the largest employed groups, since wages tended to grow more slowly than the productivity of the economy. The latter phenomenon was partially offset by the emphasis in social spending on education, health and urban services.

The debt crisis and its consequences

In the 1980s, Latin America entered the longest and most severe and widespread crisis since the Great Depression of the 1930s. This crisis was caused by a complex set of factors, prominent among which, despite the decisive weight of external forces, were the inadequacies and excesses of national economic policies. One of the most alarming aspects of the crisis was the large number and different characteristics of the economies affected by it. Another aspect was the extent of the deterioration that occurred simultaneously in most of the economic indicators. Yet another was the length of the crisis: the countries of the region are still trying to recover from it.

The crisis caused a sudden decline in economic activity, an increase in unemployment and a drop in real wages, while prices continued climbing at ever-faster rates to unprecedented heights. Consequently, the per capita product in Latin America declined significantly, falling at the end of the decade to a level lower than what the level had been in 1980, which qualified this period to be called a "lost decade." Naturally, the most negative indicators were in the external sector, characterized by serious balance of payments crises, sudden exchange rate increases and a substantial depletion of international reserves, not to mention the crushing weight of the external debt service.

---

[29] J. Ramos, *Más allá de la Economía – Más allá de la Utopía,* CIEPLAN, 1991.

The extraordinary depth and extent of the crisis become even more obvious when viewed against the backdrop of the economic development of the countries of the region in the postwar era. The point has already been made that between 1950 and 1980, the gross domestic product of the region as a whole grew at an average annual rate of 5.5 percent, which means that the gross domestic product increased five times over in this period, with even more accelerated growth in industrial production—which increased sixfold—and in capital formation.

In addition to its serious economic consequences, this phenomenon also included the difficulties encountered with the development strategy that many Latin American countries had adopted to a greater or lesser extent in the preceding decade, after the first hike in oil prices. As mentioned above, the Latin American countries took advantage of the unusual conditions in the world economic arena, especially in the financial field, to obtain large, ever-increasing amounts of foreign resources. This strategy had several positive aspects. Thanks to the inflow of these resources and also to the steady growth of its exports, Latin America was largely able to mitigate the impact of the world recession of 1974-1975 and to increase the volume of its imports as well as its economic growth rate between 1976-1980, considerably freeing its economic performance from the trend of the external cycle. Naturally, on the negative side was the extraordinary increase in the external indebtedness of the countries of the region and the rapid escalation of their current account deficits. Thus, maintaining the rate of growth depended increasingly upon the possibility of obtaining growing volumes of foreign resources as well as continuing to expand the volume of exports.

Difficulties with the prevailing development strategy

It was under these circumstances that Latin America was hit by the crisis. Its impact was felt in three major areas. The first and most traditional was the deterioration of the terms of trade; second, the spectacular rise in the real level of interest rates; and third, the sudden drop in net capital inflows. Although these three external factors were decisive in initiating the crisis, its length and depth were determined in each instance by the policies followed by the countries themselves. To better understand the origin of the crisis it will be helpful to pause briefly to analyze its causes, both external and internal.

The early 1970s marked a turning point in the long expansive phase through which the industrialized countries had passed in the postwar era. Despite the fact that economic activity rebounded somewhat after the first oil crisis, it was far from recovering the momentum it had in the long postwar period, and the rates of inflation

Deterioration of the terms of trade

and unemployment were climbing to dangerous levels. The effects of the second oil price increase on the industrialized countries were far more severe and the response of their economic policy was also very different, in that it was much more emphatically oriented toward reducing imports than before, with a consequent revival of protectionist practices and a sharp drop in the volume of international trade. For Latin America, this trend was extremely negative, so much so that in 1977-1983 the terms of trade of the non-oil-exporting countries suffered a deterioration of 38 percent, falling to a level lower than the one recorded in the depression of the 1930s.

Interest rate increases

The second factor was the sudden high cost of foreign credit. Because of the priority the industrialized countries assigned to containing inflation by controlling the money supply, and the persistent deficits in their public finances, interest rates rose sharply in 1978, reaching, in real terms, the highest levels recorded since the Great Depression (in contrast with what happened mid-way through the preceding decade, when the real interest rate was constantly negative). This increase, by halting the recovery of the industrialized economies, reduced the demand for Latin American exports, and by increasing the external debt service created a massive transfer of resources to the exterior, with a consequent increase in the current account deficit. Thus, as interest rates increased six times, Latin America's annual interest payments climbed from $6.9 billion in 1977 to over $39 billion in 1982.

The cutback in capital flows

The sudden cutback in the flow of foreign resources was the factor that contributed most to the worsening of the crisis. In recent years, representatives of the creditor banks and the IMF had been insisting that although the Latin American countries were experiencing difficulties, the banks would continue granting new credits to avoid a pro-cyclical effect. Thus, it was a matter of grave concern when, in 1982 and 1983, the granting of loans was suspended after a period of extraordinarily liberal credit, with the resulting pro-cyclical effect this decision had. The magnitude of this contraction, together with the sudden rise in interest payments due to the higher rates, dramatically reversed the direction of the transfer of resources between Latin America and the rest of the world. In fact, after the region had obtained a record amount of nearly $38 billion in 1981, as compared with an average of $5 billion a year between 1970 and 1974, around 1983 the flow of foreign resources dropped back to the levels recorded at the beginning of the preceding decade. The combined effect of the increase in interest rates and in the debt service, on the one hand, and the cessation of the flow of foreign resources and the terms of trade deterioration on the other, forced the region to transfer abroad an average of $15-20 billion a year for the rest of the decade.

Naturally, in the gestation and development of the crisis that Latin America experienced—and is still experiencing—as a result of the debt problem, there were contributing factors of an internal nature. Of course, their influence differed significantly from country to country, depending on the relative weight and specific nature of these factors. Two of the elements with the greatest impact on the problem were, on the one hand, the extraordinarily expansionist spending policies followed by some of the countries before and during this period and, on the other, the implementation of monetarist policies aimed at comprehensive trade liberalization. Although both types of policies reflected widely varying ideological stances, they both tended to increase the dependence of the respective countries on external indebtedness. More specifically, four factors that contributed significantly to the worsening of the crisis should be identified: the excesses committed in the area of foreign indebtedness; the disproportionate increase in domestic spending; the inflexibility of the stabilization policies and the exchange lag; and the accelerated deregulation of the internal financial system and the rise in real interest rates.

Internal factors

During this period, faced with the necessity of correcting their external imbalances, amending their faulty exchange rate policies, slowing their inflationary processes, and servicing or reducing the debt, the Latin American countries began to implement adjustment policies (aimed at external imbalances), stabilization policies (related to the fight against inflation), and debt management policies.

The basic objective of the adjustment policies was to eliminate those portions of the current account deficit that could no longer be financed with foreign resources or international reserves. To accomplish this, the countries applied in different ways two types of policies: policies to control aggregate demand—including fiscal, monetary and income policy—and policies aimed at raising the relative price of tradable goods, including exchange rate, tariff and export promotion policies. In reality aimed at raising the relative price of tradable goods, these policies tended to fall within the scope of the basic agreements concluded with the IMF to obtain loans. These agreements generally set limits for the expansion of the international assets of the central banks and for the internal and external indebtedness of the public sector, stipulating that the governments would have to reduce their deficits by raising taxes, increasing the rates of public enterprises and cutting current expenditures. It was also generally agreed that during the adjustment process the real exchange rate would be adjusted upward, real wages would be lowered and positive real interest rates would be maintained.

As mentioned above, since the strictness and tenacity with which these policies were applied varied greatly from country to country, they had varying degrees of success in achieving their basic objectives. Generally, greater progress was made when more attention was paid to reducing external imbalances than to controlling inflation. Moreover, these policies had a very high social cost, which is another of the legacies with which the structural reforms and economic growth strategies promoted by the countries in recent years have had to contend.

Management of the external debt problem

The external debt crisis in Latin America created the necessary conditions for a potential international financial collapse similar to others that have occurred in the past, thus signaling the end of the upward phases of the growth cycle and of the flow of resources from the developed to the developing countries, processes which have been brilliantly described by Kindleberger.[30] In 1982, U.S. bank loans to Latin American countries equaled 124 percent of their capital. This figure increased to 200 percent in the case of the country's nine largest banking institutions, which gives an idea of the vulnerability of the international financial system at this time and of the risk to which the system was exposed to in this part of the world. In addition, the outstanding international loans at the time of the depression in the 1930s were generally financed with bonds purchased by private investors, which affected only their own equity.

After 1982, however, the suspension of payments by certain Latin American countries would have seriously compromised the solvency of various large international banks, and, given the close relationship that exists between the financial systems of the northern countries, this would have also led to the destabilization of world banking, with unpredictable results for the level of production and trade in the developed economies. Nevertheless, in reality, the international financial system demonstrated a surprising ability to

---

[30] C. Kindleberger, *Manias, Panics and Crashes,* 1978, and *Keynesianism versus Monetarism and Other Essays in Financial History,* 1985.

adapt and thus avoided collapse, despite an extremely severe payments crisis in most of the Latin American countries, in addition to others in Africa, Asia and Eastern Europe. Moreover, in the midst of the crisis, the creditor banks even managed to increase their profitability. This was reflected positively in their balance sheets and it helped them to effect a dramatic reduction in their capital commitments in the Latin American countries, which were cut in half between 1982 and 1987.

The most important measure the financial system used to survive this challenge consisted of an unprecedented level of coordinated international management. The main component of this collective management was the action of the IMF, which negotiated adjustment programs with the debtor countries on a case-by-case basis, giving the "green light" for the restructuring of bank debts on commercial terms. The governments of the OECD aided this process by rescheduling the debts they had contracted through the Paris Club, promoting negotiations between private banks and debtors with the participation of the Fund, and granting bilateral loans to supplement the contributions of the IMF and the commercial banks.

What is even more interesting is that this strategy was modified as time went on, with respect to both the management of the debt problem and the adjustment and economic restructuring policies in Latin America. ECLAC recently identified three stages in the evolution of this strategy.[31]

The first of these stages is characterized by the search for areas of agreement between creditors and debtors, and by the coordinated international management of the problem, primarily among the former. Creditors and debtors quite naturally tend to approach the debt service problem from different perspectives. Creditors demand a strict adjustment of the current account of the debtor countries' balance of payments so that they can regularly service their debt without the need for new credits. Debtors, of course, wish to protect their country's production and income and, at least in the short term, prefer new loans to making adjustments. The negotiations between the two parties can produce acceptable solutions, but such negotiations are usually difficult. Thus, default became one component of the solutions, as well as a reduction in the market value of debt instruments, which forced creditors to share the costs of excessive credits.

Phase one: coordinated international management

---

[31] CEPAL, *La evolución del problema de la deuda externa en América Latina y el Caribe,* Santiago, Chile, 1988.

In 1982, various factors made this route inadvisable. First, the growth of the world economy had provided considerable experience in the matter of the international coordination of policies and the handling of systemic problems such as the debt crisis. Second, the debt had been documented through instruments that were difficult to sell, which at first delayed the fall of their price in the market. Finally, an institutional infrastructure with an enormous mobilization capability had been created to prevent default, thus enabling the many parties involved in the problem—private banks, creditor governments, multilateral organizations and debtor countries—to confer and to agree on some type of transaction. The existence of this institutional infrastructure provided an unparalleled opportunity to negotiate agreements between creditors and debtors.

To accomplish this, however, a major obstacle had to be overcome: the payment problems of the Latin American countries were so critical that postponing repayment of the principal was not enough; instead, it was necessary to reschedule the interest payments. The banks could not accept this and the multilateral financial institutions did not have the resources necessary to make it possible. The IMF, however, played a decisive and innovative role in this dilemma, acting as an intermediary between creditors and debtors to work out an agreement between the two parties that would take into account the interests of the creditors regarding adjustment policies and of the debtors in obtaining new financing. In this context, the IMF insisted that the banks agree to grant new loans (called nonvoluntary loans) to help finance the programs it approved and a portion—which in fact was approximately half—of the interest payments.

The second stage, from 1985 to 1987, was characterized by the divergence of interests and the end of cooperation. In the preceding phase, three rescheduling rounds had taken place. Although some progress was made, there were disappointments as well. The IMF did not always obtain the expected input of funds from the large creditor banks, and the latter failed to line up the smaller banks, which were the first to be excluded from the new credits. The debtors complained not only about the sacrifices involved in the adjustment but also about the high financing costs of the rescheduling, and they began to express doubts about whether the communication between the banks constituted a form of collective crisis management or a cartel of creditors whose aim was to give the advantage to the banks by spreading the costs of solving this problem. In 1984 the debtor countries reacted by establishing lines of communication among themselves, initially through the Quito Declaration, which came into being at a conference convened by the President of Ecuador, Oswaldo

Phase two: international management and nonvoluntary resources

Hurtado, with the support of ECLAC and SELA, and later through the group that formed the Cartagena Consensus, which included eleven countries and became the official forum for the debtors.

The major contribution expected from the banks in this new stage consisted once again of new nonvoluntary loans to provide general support for the balance of payments of the debtor countries. The banks' accession to the new agreements was based on the fear of their vulnerability to potential defaults, the expectation of a sustained recovery of the world economy, the idea that the debtors were besieged by cash flow problems and not insolvency, and confidence that the IMF would be able to enforce the adjustment policies. The slight decline in interest rates and the nascent recovery of the economy of the United States justified these expectations. Nevertheless, all of these variables evolved in such a way that the willingness of the banks to participate actively and consistently in new nonvoluntary loan agreements waned. The main objective of this strategy—obtaining new nonvoluntary credits to finance structural reforms and economic growth in the debtor countries—suffered irreversible setbacks as a result of the considerable increase in the reserves of the creditor banks, which allayed their fears about their financial vulnerability, and the increasingly negative opinion these institutions were forming about the region's future ability to pay, i.e., its solvency.

The experiences and dissatisfactions mentioned above opened the door to a new stage, characterized by a list of market options. The divergence of interests among the protagonists of the crisis blurred first the outlines of the strategy of collective management of the problem and then the possibility of obtaining better terms and new financing through greater concerted efforts on the part of the debtors. In these circumstances, the banks began to propose a range of options other than assuming greater risks in Latin America, which meant that even the goals of the Baker Plan concerning the amount of new credits (considered insufficient by many analysts) were beyond reach. These proposals consisted basically of market options and were aimed at cleaning up the banks' credit portfolios in Latin America without the necessity of making nonvoluntary loans. The new options had two basic criteria as their common denominator: they had to be based on the performance of the market and they had to be negotiated voluntarily between creditors and debtors. They included, basically, the following solutions:

• Credits for investment projects and commercial activities that could offer the banks a greater inducement than general credits (considered more risky) and thus be more likely to provide a return.

Phase three:
the Brady Plan

- Onlending, or programs allowing banks to redistribute some of their credits in the debtor country's market.
- Issue of bonds by the debtor country, probably with priority over older debts, totally or partially eliminating the need for new nonvoluntary credits.
- Convertible external debt notes delivered by the debtor countries to the banks for conversion into share capital in the countries.
- Exit bonds, whereby a portion of the outstanding debt is converted into fixed interest bonds that allow the banks to "exit" the process of rescheduling and granting new credits.
- Conversion of debt into capital, effected directly by the banks or through transactions in the secondary market.
- Conversion of debt into beneficent funds, channeled through nonprofit institutions, which denominate it in the currency of the debtor country and use it for philanthropic purposes.
- Capitalization of the interest on the debt through voluntary negotiations of limited scope.
- Loans for general balance of payments support, supposedly coordinated with bilateral or multilateral public loan operations.

The introduction of the Brady Plan to solve the debt problem was a very important step toward a type of agreement that revived past hopes of the developing countries, particularly the Latin American countries.

The most important was undoubtedly the introduction of the principal and/or interest reduction principle, through solutions arrived at jointly by the debtor country and its bank creditors.

Mexico initiated the process through a successful debt refinancing program that was later emulated by Costa Rica, Venezuela and Uruguay. At this point in time, Argentina and Brazil are well on their way to concluding agreements, while Ecuador has for several months been pursuing similar goals. An evaluation of the solutions to the bank debt problem should consider not only the reduction of principal and interest but also to what extent these solutions serve as the basis for building international financial credibility, facilitate access to the capital markets, and promote foreign investment and the return of capital transferred abroad.

Recently, the Enterprise for the Americas Initiative took a significant step by creating a facility to reduce the public debt of the countries of the region with the United States government, which so far has been utilized by Nicaragua, Honduras, Jamaica and Bolivia. In addition, the Canadian government has begun a welcome process of forgiving the official public debt of the Caribbean countries.

The conclusion to be drawn from these steady advances in reducing Latin American debt, as well as the progress made in the Paris Club with regard to commercial debt, lead me to believe that without ignoring the serious impact of the external debt problem on the region, some countries, as a result of the nine mechanisms described above, have begun to manage the debt problem in a manner more consistent with the need to sustain adequate levels of development.

In the final analysis, the general principle is confirmed: no effective way out of the problem will be found without speeding up the growth rate of the gross domestic product and the exports of the debtor countries.

From adjustment policies to structural reforms

Chapter III

The region's problems in the nineties

Twenty years after the Prebisch Report, the world is radically changed. Contributing to this change are the three decades of unprecedented prosperity that began in the postwar years, during which time the industrialized countries experienced an average annual growth rate of 5 percent and their production quadrupled, while world trade grew 50 percent more rapidly and multiplied six times. The accelerated growth of trade, the exporting of U.S. technology and capital to countries whose economies were destroyed by the war, and the expansion of transnational companies made possible by this process gave rise to an increasingly interdependent and integrated world economy.

Changes in the world

　　The most important changes, however, were qualitative. A century dominated by the same industries, technologies and energy sources (oil and petrochemicals, steel and the internal combustion engine, transportation and durable goods), and controlled by the same countries and primary sectors, has come to an end as we enter a new world in which other countries, sectors, products and technologies are interacting. A new technological paradigm holds, based on information, microelectronics and knowledge in general, while the world economy for the first time is not so narrowly dependent on labor and natural resources. The traditional relationship between production and finances is also changing—so much so that the value of international capital movements is fifteen times greater than the value of world trade. All of this has profoundly changed productive structures, the configuration of the work force, social preferences, demand, the composition of the gross domestic product, the ways in which companies operate, and the role of services therein, with particular emphasis on information and communications. Latin America could not be left out of this process of change.

　　Partly because of these changes, but even more as a result of endogenous causes, Latin America has also changed. A brief summary of some of the concepts mentioned above regarding this transformation will be helpful. Between 1950 and 1980, the region's gross domestic product grew at an average annual rate of 5.5 percent, which was higher than the rate attained by other developing areas and slightly above the growth rate of the industrialized countries. This growth was accompanied by a relatively intense process of investment, and productive and technological change. The region's industrial capacity was expanded and diversified, making it possible to satisfy with domestic production almost all the demand for consumer goods and a growing percentage of capital goods. The steady advances in infrastructure development greatly facilitated the integration and sectoral interdependence of the Latin American economies, which, after the crisis, was to become a very important consideration in their restructuring or reform.

The 1973 oil crisis and the successive recessions the world economy was then enduring hit the region hard. Nevertheless, the rebirth of the international capital markets, made possible by the anti-recession policies of the industrial nations and the deposits of petrodollars in private banks, allowed the countries of the region to avoid the impact of the crisis for several years by utilizing foreign credit. In doing so, the Latin American countries merely took advantage of the opportunities provided by the prevailing extraordinary climate of international financial permissiveness to mitigate the effects of the crisis, without realizing that they were compromising their future. It could be said, then, that the seventies represented the true turning point on the road to development sought by the Latin American countries in the postwar period, and that with the erosion of the discipline of development, they prepared the way for the lost decade.

In the early 1980s, the sudden rise in interest rates, the drying up of foreign capital flows and the long-term decline in the terms of trade thrust the region into the worst crisis the world had seen since the Great Depression of the thirties. The rest of the decade was dominated by a succession of more or less unilateral or coordinated strategies aimed at managing the debt problem, and by the implementation of a series of adjustment policies designed to curb imports, expand exports and obtain the foreign resources the economies needed to satisfy their limited import requirements and to service the debt.

After the long process of transformation and development in Latin America during the postwar period, and the external debt crisis and sacrifices necessitated by the adjustment policies of the 1980s, the Latin American countries, using various approaches, began to intensively apply measures responding for the most part to domestic needs, but also taking external considerations into account. These measures departed from the traditional view of Latin American development and were aimed at overcoming the inherent limitations of the adjustment policies that had been followed until then.

Most leaders and experts as well as the public believed that these measures were based primarily on the perceptions of the economic authorities of the developed countries and the multilateral financial organizations, which had a large presence in Latin America. With the passage of time, responses to the debt crisis evolved from the implementation of monetary adjustment policies to the introduction of more expansive structural reforms; from measures aimed solely at ensuring service of the debt to greater concern for economic growth and reduction of the debt; from a preponderant emphasis on the financial position of the creditor banks to more concern for the recovery of the debtor countries; from coordinated management of the debt problem, primarily by the creditor banks, to other methods that assigned a significant role first to the IMF and later to the World Bank; from the relative exclusion of the monetary authorities of the creditor countries to their greater involvement in the solution of the problem; and from strategies that included only the parties directly involved in the problem—creditors and debtors—to an array of market solutions.

Structural reforms

In these responses, it is difficult to separate the influence of the creditor countries, primarily the United States, from the initiatives of the Latin American countries. Consequently, the origin of this series of reforms is not entirely clear. Although at one time an attempt was made to label them the "Washington Consensus," it is not wholly accurate, not only because these reforms were generally the result of very specific national needs and initiatives but also because the Latin American countries, as already mentioned, began to experiment with liberalization and openness as far back as the 1960s.

In any case, these responses were not formulated unilaterally by U.S. banking institutions or the international financial organizations, but were rather a combination—in arguable proportions—of their recommendations and the economic modernization and trade liberalization initiatives undertaken at various stages by the Latin American countries themselves. Moreover, this was not a generally accepted name but rather a handy label applied to this particular set of prescriptions by an institution and one of its writers.[32] It was really

The true origin of the reforms

---

[32] The Institute for International Economics and one of its most distinguished researchers, John Williamson.

just a useful means of easily identifying the series of measures proposed to the Latin American countries in recent years. It would seem more appropriate to conclude that these measures were being developed in response to the gradual emergence of a Latin American political and economic consensus.

Another interesting aspect of this consensus, apart from its institutional origins, is its conceptual history. The new strategy implicit in this series of measures owed its existence partly to the obsolescence of the development model the Latin American countries had followed in the postwar era, partly to the weariness of the industrialized countries with respect to foreign aid—which was a major component of the conventional model mentioned above—and partly to a general loss of interest in development theory.

There is another reason why, in academic circles, development theory was ignored and had seemingly become irrelevant, especially in the North, but also among Latin American economists whose responsibility was to help formulate economic policies aimed at alleviating the crisis in the short term. Basically, the Washington Consensus was more than a set of new ideas and recommendations; it represented the return of the strong influence that "mainstream economics" had always exerted in our countries over and above the alternatives proposed by Latin American development theory.

In recent years a considerable degree of consensus has been achieved in Latin America concerning the origins of and solutions to the crisis it experienced in the eighties, a consensus that emerged from the lessons the Latin American countries learned at so high a cost.

Above all, the causes and the nature of the crisis are more clear today. Unlike the period immediately following the crisis, today there is a clearer understanding of its most fundamental aspects: the role of both external and internal factors in igniting the crisis; whether it was a short- or long-term phenomenon; whether it was basically a financial problem or should be viewed primarily as an economic growth issue; the nature of the measures implemented to deal with it; and the need to replace recessionary adjustment policies and to institute structural reforms geared more toward renewed economic growth. It is also clear that these reforms should not focus solely on the recovery of macroeconomic balances, an essential but not exclusive condition for development, but should go further and include policies aimed at vigorously promoting development. Naturally, unanimity is more difficult to achieve when the objective is to advance from a series of general recommendations, which could apparently be implemented uniformly, to the adaptation of each rec-

The growing economic consensus

ommendation to the specific needs of each country. Growth policies are more in need of such adaptation than are policies related to overall balances. For the reasons given, it is also difficult to agree on the pace, sequence and amount of time required to implement such reforms. It follows, then, that the countries themselves are better qualified to make the necessary adjustments than are the multilateral organizations.

This modest but significant progress toward a Latin American economic consensus would not have been possible without a new political consensus. The same is certainly true of the inward-oriented development policies followed by the countries of the region in the postwar period. The emergence of this new political consensus coincided with the fall from power—for the most diverse reasons—of various governments with a populist or ideological political orientation, characterized by confrontation and conflict, and by poor discipline or extremism. As they were replaced, a new civic philosophy evolved, one that was more realistic and pragmatic, less impatient and more mature, less inclined toward aggression and more willing to seek areas of agreement, more removed from extremes and more moderately oriented. Less political impatience and a renewed emphasis on moderation, stability and consensus made it easier for the leaders to effect reforms that would have been impossible in a different political context. Therefore, just as our economic leaders have realized that our development strategies must be modernized, so must our political leaders accept these new truths.

Toward a new political consensus

A dynamic political consensus is taking shape in many countries concerning the requirements and aims of economic reform, sustained in the long term by the ability of the new model to respond to the region's extraordinary social conditions.

Economic reforms are legitimized politically by their effectiveness in the social sphere. In the difficult adjustment period, however, this consensus depends largely on society's perception of the fairness of the adjustment burden and the promise that today's austerity holds for tomorrow. Consequently, the consensus must be reinforced by the provision of high-quality public services, an effective reflection of social communication and skillful government, which will be put to the test in such difficult and challenging circumstances.

How can the Latin American crisis of the 1980s be explained? My opinion, after observing the development of Latin America from the vantage point of ECLA and in my own country prior to assuming my current responsibilities at the IDB, is that the main causes of the crisis stemmed from a combination of three

The three main causes of the crisis

problems: first, the structural management of the economies of the region in recent decades; second, of course, the external debt problem; and, third, events in the international arena.

Regarding the first of these problems, the economic policies of the Latin American countries were vitiated by three basic errors. The first was distortion of the price system, which tended to occur in a number of mixed economies such as those that prevailed in the region during this long period, and the excessive tolerance of the inflationary process that characterized their political and economic systems, together with a series of overly specific and not always well-conceived redistributive policies, which, to make matters worse, fueled inflation. These biases affected key prices, interest rates and exchange rates more than they did the rest of the economy. The second was excessive confidence in the import substitution process. Of course, we are all conquering heroes after the battle, but at the time everyone believed that these policies were necessary and only a few questioned whether they were right or wrong. It is also true that once the easy stage of the import substitution process was over, this policy was subjected to growing criticism, which led to the first trade liberalization experiments in the 1960s, primarily in Brazil, Colombia and Chile. It is widely recognized that the Latin American countries had excessively closed economies, that they missed out on the business opportunities that were opening up in some sectors in the 1960s and 1970s, and that they are just now emerging from this process and moving toward greater openness to foreign trade. Finally, the question arises of economic voluntarism and the high degree of confidence placed in the State as the promoter and originator of economic growth. This confidence was justified in the postwar era, but, later, the cost and inefficiency of excessive State intervention in the most diverse affairs and the need to place more trust in market mechanisms became obvious. Albert Hirschman pointed out some time ago that one of the biggest mistakes that we Latin Americans made was to ask our governments to do more than they were capable of doing. At the same time, the discriminatory potential of State intervention, together with the power accumulated by special interest groups in societies well into the development and internal coordination process, created the paradoxical situation in which many of the policies implemented in some of the poorest sectors ended up benefiting high-income groups and the bureaucrats themselves.

As a result, our development patterns were characterized by those elements which, in my opinion, clearly exemplify the difficulties the region has encountered in its recent history: our development was unstable, inefficient and inequitable. The instability was related to the financial performance of the private sector and to excessive government tolerance of inflationary pressures, which, at a certain point, became uncontrollable and brought many countries to the brink of hyperinflation. The inefficiency was associated in particular with excessive protectionism and the isolation of the region due to its lack of international competitiveness, while economies in other parts of the world were turning increasingly toward global interdependence and trade. The inequity was caused by institutions and mechanisms that had a highly concentrating effect on the distribution of income, resulting in unprecedented levels of extreme poverty, a condition rooted in our colonial past that still oppressed a third of Latin America's population and which the development policies of the postwar period had failed to eradicate.

The other problem, as indicated in the preceding chapter, was external indebtedness, with its pervasive consequences and its profound domestic and international implications. In fact, the critical aspects mentioned above were exacerbated by the easy credit the countries of the region availed themselves of in the seventies to offset the effects of the oil crises and the worldwide recession, thus delaying even further the solution of a number of problems left over from the past. These problems were severely intensified in the 1980s when the world instituted a policy of fighting inflation, the consequences of which were a sudden rise in interest rates, a sharp contraction of credit and a precipitous fall in the terms of trade of the developing countries, particularly those of Latin America.

The external debt problem

The consequences are well known; in the eighties the region transferred more than $223 billion abroad to service the debt and pay dividends on foreign investments, while at the same time witnessing a sudden drop in the inflow of foreign capital and an unprecedented deterioration of its terms of trade, all of which meant an enormous restriction of the entire region's investment and growth potential.

When the crisis exploded in 1982, most Latin American countries chose to make greater sacrifices in order to continue servicing the debt, and none of them wanted—openly at least—to consider default, as they might have done in the past. The governments remembered very clearly, first of all, that in situations such as the Great Depression, most of their external debt was in bonds sold in the international capital markets in a highly dispersed manner, which lowered the cost of the moratorium to the holders of such bonds and limited the latter's ability to respond. They also remembered that, in any case, most of the moratoriums had led to reprisals that excluded them from the international financial markets for several decades. The wholesale transfer of funds that this approach entailed not only exerted almost unbearable pressure on the balance of payments but also distorted the internal allocation of resources and severely curtailed the funds available for investment and, hence, the momentum of economic growth.

The extraordinary level of interest rates in the following years was a determining factor in the worsening of this problem. It was further intensified by the sudden contraction in the flow of foreign credit and the drastic deterioration of the terms of trade of Latin American export products. Another disturbing factor related to the first two was the massive capital flight caused by high international interest rates. Gross domestic investment fell in real terms from 24 percent of GDP in 1974-1980 to 16 percent in the 1983-1990 period, a trend which does not bode well for the future. Another consequence of the crisis was the deterioration of the region's physical and institutional infrastructure. It is extremely discouraging to compare the promising, sustained growth rates recorded in Latin America in the sixties and seventies of roughly 5-6 percent per annum with an annual decrease of one percent of the gross domestic product starting with the outbreak of the crisis.

The international economic environment

Finally, it would be difficult to exaggerate the influence of the international economic environment on the policies of the Latin American countries and the success of their structural reforms. It should be noted in this regard that the growth of the international economy was affected in recent years by persistent recessionary signals. Starting in the early eighties, as a result of the increase in the prices of oil and other basic products, inflation accelerated in a number of industrialized countries. These countries reacted to the inflationary threat by implementing monetary policies that led to the contraction of credit and a sudden rise in interest rates. This change in turn slowed economic growth and raised unemployment. These trends, as mentioned above, had a devastating effect on the terms of trade of the developing countries. The deterioration was worse than it was in the Great Depression; in fact, between 1980 and 1986, the terms of trade of basic products fell approximately 40 percent, compared with the 30 percent decline recorded between 1929 and 1932. Moreover, while the developed countries had long insisted on the need for Latin America to liberalize its trade regulations, the world trade system was becoming increasingly closed.

The international community is not sufficiently aware of the efforts and achievements of the Latin American countries in this area. Its attention has been distracted, first, by the trend toward the formation of trade blocs and the concentration of trade within certain areas. Second, attention has been focused on the prospects of consolidation of the European Community in 1992 and the political and economic reforms underway in Eastern Europe. Not only does the international community know little about Latin America's efforts to open its economies but, what is worse, the global economy is not supporting these efforts. Perhaps the most fundamental requirement of structural reform is a more favorable international economic environment, characterized essentially by a higher global growth rate, growth in the markets of the industrialized countries, and the increasing liberalization of international trade. Unfortunately, this is not happening.

As a result of the problems mentioned above, and despite its own efforts, the outlook for Latin America in the 1980s was very negative. The growth of the gross domestic product has been minimal in recent years and the standard of living of the average Latin American is now the same as it was in 1977, which means that much more than a single decade was lost. The largest countries of the region that have had negative experiences, such as Argentina and Brazil, influenced this average considerably, but there are many other countries that also recorded declines, although not as dramatic, in their overall production. Inflation once again became endemic in Latin America, although the importance of economic stability to the well-being of the population and as a policy objective was later widely recognized and substantial efforts were made to combat this scourge. The levels of Latin American external debt have remained relatively stable in the last three years, reaching some $423 billion in 1990. This caused a constant, although perhaps decreasing, net transfer of financial resources to the creditor countries totaling approximately $15-20 billion between 1983 and 1989, with a decrease at the end of the period due primarily to increased capital inflows. In 1990 this transfer became positive once again.

A persistently negative outlook

Added to the negative effect of the transfer of financial resources on the balance of payments was its impact on the fiscal accounts, which was made even worse by the State's assumption of obligations originally contracted by the private sector. At the same time, growing trade surpluses, because they were not merged with fiscal resources, were monetized and created inflationary pressures, causing overvaluation of the exchange rate, financial speculation, capital flight, and a lack of confidence in economic policy.

What is structural reform?

Nature of the structural reforms

The growing perception of how best to deal with the debt crisis was based on fiscal austerity, the liberalization of domestic markets and the opening of the economy. To achieve these objectives, a series of structural reforms was proposed. These reforms differed substantially from the principles of the structuralist view: import substitution, orientation toward the domestic market, various forms of tariff, fiscal or exchange rate protection (or discrimination), redistributive programs subsidized by the government, State intervention and planning, and excessive public expenditures. The new economic policy objectives depended fundamentally on the free operation of the markets. In this connection, the term "structural reforms" began to be used to refer to a set of measures aimed at liberalizing domestic markets, privatizing State enterprises and certain social services, and opening the economies to international trade and private capital inflows.

The "Washington Consensus"

At a conference on the subject in 1989, John Williamson listed ten areas in which the structural reforms were concentrated.[33] The country studies presented in this conference tried to give an idea of the extent to which national viewpoints on these subjects coincided with what the publisher of Williamson's book called the "Washington Consensus."

These studies focused on several groupings, including Bolivia, Chile and Peru, considered as three experiments in policies; Brazil, Mexico and Argentina, the largest debtors of the region; Colombia and Venezuela; and the Caribbean and Central American countries. The principal common denominators are discussed below.

Fiscal discipline

First, fiscal discipline emerges as the key aspect since deficits are the primary source of macroeconomic distortions, in the form of inflationary processes, payment deficits and capital flight. This position does not exclude the possibility of cautiously applying Keynesian expansionist policies in certain cases and for as long as necessary. Nor does it imply ignoring the negative effects of fiscal austerity such as social costs or a declining gross domestic product. Nevertheless, it does stress the importance of two subjects; namely, that the effects of an expansionist or recessionary fiscal policy are

---

[33] J. Williamson, *Latin American Adjustment: How Much Has Happened?*, Washington, D.C., Institute for International Economics, 1990. This book is a collection of studies presented at a conference organized by the Institute in Washington, D.C. in November, 1989.

short-lived, especially in a context of sharp fiscal restrictions, and that carrying a huge deficit erodes confidence to such an extent that it becomes the most influential factor in discouraging private investment.

A distinct change can be observed in the attitudes of politicians, economists and even the electorate, from one of general indifference toward the size of the fiscal deficit and its inflationary effects to a strong commitment to fiscal discipline and price stability. In some countries, such as Chile, this new awareness occurred sooner. In others (Brazil and Peru), it was slower than average. In fact, substantial progress was made in this area by Bolivia, Colombia, Costa Rica, Chile, Jamaica and Mexico. In Bolivia, the fiscal deficit as a percentage of GDP was reduced from 27 percent in 1984 to 6 percent in 1988, and in Mexico a deficit of 7.4 percent of GDP in 1982 was converted into a surplus of 7.4 percent in 1988.

Although there are sharp differences of opinion about what fiscal discipline means, as well as pressures to relax it to attain various objectives such as increased social spending, there is a general awareness of the importance of keeping the fiscal deficit and inflation under control and taking a firmer approach to this subject.

The second area refers to the ordering of public spending priorities. The more conservative sectors believe that cutting public expenditures is a more effective way of reducing fiscal deficits than raising taxes. The first items that come to mind when discussing expenditures are the military budget, government services and various types of subsidies, especially those of a discriminatory nature. Usually excluded from this category are investment expenditures and those oriented toward the poorest segments of the population. Thus, expenditures for infrastructure, for health and education programs and for the poorest groups of the population usually meet with everyone's approval. This attitude facilitates agreement among all sectors of the population. An effective policy in this area would consist, then, of maintaining strict control over public spending and shaping it in such a way as to benefit "the future and the most disadvantaged." Only four countries seem to have succeeded in significantly reducing public expenditures as a percentage of GDP: Bolivia, Chile, Jamaica and Mexico. The advances made in this area, therefore, are less relevant than in the field of fiscal discipline. It is interesting to note, regarding one of the ideas mentioned above, the differences between the position of the IMF, which favors an overall reduction of public expenditures, and that of the World Bank, which not only monitors macroeconomic balances but also keeps an eye on growth and is more involved in national decisions concerning certain

Controlling public expenditures

investments, in which the public sector usually still plays an important role. For this reason, I mentioned earlier that the measures proposed by the "Washington Consensus" are more applicable to the maintenance of macroeconomic balances than to the promotion of economic growth, which requires that national and sectoral needs and differences be taken into account.

Improvement of the tax system

Another aspect is the tax system, for which some experts advocate the widest possible base and effective collection procedures, while opposing a highly progressive tax system. The reforms suggested at this stage of Latin American development are unanimous in their acceptance of the notion that an efficient tax system depends primarily on taxing a very large base, establishing relatively simple rules, instituting efficient collection and audit procedures, and setting moderate upper and lower marginal rates. This point of view is not shared by groups interested in preserving tax brackets or categories or those who support highly progressive taxes as a means of redistributing income. Perhaps the newest perception in the current thinking is that expansion of the tax base is probably the most effective method of reconciling and achieving the objectives of adequate collection and progressivity.

This approach is gaining acceptance in Latin America, where Bolivia, Colombia, Chile and Jamaica have already instituted reforms aimed at simplifying the system and expanding the tax base, as well as lower upper margins and the utilization of new indirect systems. Other countries are currently moving in this direction. Mexico, for example, has made an interesting effort to close the loopholes in corporate taxes. Another problem these reforms must tackle is the heavy erosion of tax receipts caused by the prevailing high rates of inflation, a problem whose solution depends on the curbing of inflation or, in special cases, the indexing of taxes, as in Brazil. The taxation of interest earned on capital transferred abroad is another problem that will require both legislation making such interest taxable and international agreements for the exchange of information needed to track such capital and permit legal enforcement.

Deregulation of the financial system

Deregulation of the financial system and of interest rates is the fourth point these reforms address. On this subject, diametrically opposed pressures have also been exerted, favoring, on the one hand, excessively high real rates at the expense of economic activity and price stability, and, on the other, very low or even negative rates that discourage investment and threaten the solvency of the government and of businesses. The subject is not limited to interest rates but also includes the liberalization and deregulation of financial markets, together with an improvement in the corresponding regulatory mechanisms, as well as the elimination of existing subsidies. With some exceptions, little has been done about the latter. The regulatory systems have been strengthened in countries such as Bolivia and Chile. In various countries such as Argentina, Chile, Brazil, Mexico, Costa Rica and Colombia, there was some progress in the eighties in the sense that interest rates were determined by the market, although in Colombia there was a subsequent reversal and in Venezuela authorization was given for setting maximum rates for bank credits and minimum rates for the interest paid on deposits. The determination of interest rates by the market seems to be at the center of this type of reform.

The fifth focus of the reforms is the exchange rate, which is directly related to the new strategy based on the opening of the economies to foreign trade and aimed at export-led development. There is a growing consensus that the first requirement for the growth of exports is a competitive exchange rate, which is understood to be one that enables the economy to grow at a level commensurate with its installed capacity. There is also a tendency to believe that in order to invest in productive sectors oriented toward foreign markets, businesses must be assured that the exchange rate will remain relatively stable. Moreover, it has been established that a single exchange rate is preferable, in the long-run, to a multiple rate system. Everyone agrees that care must be taken, as some analysts have pointed out, that the devaluation or maintenance of a truly competitive exchange rate does not compromise macroeconomic balances nor involve a regressive redistribution of income through higher prices for imports, which could seriously threaten the political support for such a strategy. Currently, a number of countries such as Brazil, Colombia, Costa Rica, Chile and Mexico manage the exchange rate on a "crawling peg" or moving parity basis, while others such as Bolivia, Jamaica and Venezuela have floating or flexibly determined rates. In all cases, the exchange rates are either determined by the market or react to signals from the market. Fewer and fewer countries have multiple exchange rates or a graduated or periodic system of currency appreciation.

Management of the exchange rate

Trade liberalization—another objective of these reforms—is a necessary complement of setting competitive exchange rates. In this regard, the new strategy proposes the gradual reduction of customs tariffs and, above all, replacement of the import permit system by tariffs. Because of the crucial importance of imports of intermediate goods to exporting industries, this strategy also recommends enabling exporters to obtain a "drawback" or refund equal to the du-

Trade liberalization

ties paid on such imports. There is a wide range of opinion, both in the United States and in Latin America, concerning to what extent and at what pace the foreign trade of the Latin American countries should be liberalized. Nevertheless, most of them have moved in this direction, although at different times and speeds. Chile and Argentina had already liberalized in the seventies, although only the former managed to follow this policy consistently. Later, Bolivia, Colombia, Costa Rica, Jamaica and Mexico took this step, and Argentina, together with Venezuela, have again committed themselves to fairly drastic trade liberalization policies. One indicator of this attitude is the growing number of Latin American countries that have joined the GATT.

Direct foreign investment

The set of recommendations assigns a very important role to direct foreign investment (DFI). In fact, a trade liberalization and export promotion strategy presupposes interest in attracting rather than barring such investments. This policy should stimulate the flow of capital necessary for the growth of the export sector, and DFI, by definition, tends to be concentrated in that sector, to bring in foreign expertise and technology and, more importantly, to establish ties between the investors' markets and the recipient countries. This attitude contrasts with the view prevailing in Latin America since the late seventies, represented symbolically by Resolution 24 of the Andean Group, which was passed in those years and which signified a deepening of the import substitution strategy and the dependency theory, in an international context dominated by the crisis of the multinationals and, in general, by a vigorous process of transnationalization. This is one element of the new strategy that is still the subject of heated debate and which is closely associated with the trend toward privatization. The discussion becomes even more heated if the Latin American countries have to subsidize foreign investment through various mechanisms used to convert debt into market-priced investments (debt-equity swaps). It should be concluded in this regard that the attitude of the Latin American countries toward DFI has generally become much more favorable than it was in the past, although there still has not been a substantial increase in the flow of foreign private resources (except, for special reasons, in Mexico), due to the slower growth and prevailing situation of the world economy.

Privatization is another key area of the new policy recommendations. As successive methods were tried to manage the debt, particularly under the Baker Plan, the United States government and the multilateral organizations tried to persuade the Latin American countries of the need to privatize a considerable number of their public enterprises. The most obvious objective of this proposal was to remove the burden that the operation of these companies usually represented for the public sector and, in the process, to reduce fiscal deficits. Another no less important perception was that their transfer to the private sector would make these companies more sensitive to market signals, more oriented toward earning profits and more interested in efficient management. This topic was even more controversial than the preceding one. Although it could be shown that there is perhaps a strong current of opinion in favor of privatization, both within and outside Latin America, the criticism is focused on the methods used to carry it out. From this perspective, it is possible to question how thoroughly the process is analyzed, the pace at which it proceeds, the techniques used to determine the value of the companies, the assessment of the buyers' capabilities and, above all, the claim that privatization is a universal panacea for the external debt problems and the liberalization of the economies. In light of these criticisms, not only the authors but also the advocates of privatization can justifiably raise the possibility that this policy may be entirely discredited if the techniques used to implement it are not improved based on past experience. Great strides are being made in this area and the privatization processes currently underway are being handled much more efficiently.

The privatization of public enterprises

Deregulation—another goal of the reforms—is a predominantly U.S. trend that began during the presidency of Jimmy Carter and was greatly accelerated in the Reagan administration. The United States has since deregulated its airlines, transportation, telecommunications, natural gas production and distribution, and banking system, among others. The new series of measures proposed for Latin America includes strong recommendations in favor of this process. At first glance, this element seems consistent with the above aspects. Nevertheless, there is far less knowledge and experience in this area, as well as less emphasis on the implementation of these measures. Theoretically, or as foreign experience shows, they are at the center of any effort to reform the State along the lines mentioned above. And yet, throughout the world—and particularly in Latin America—the question of State reform remains complex and controversial, both in the field of economic theory as well as the social sciences. Consequently, the objective of promoting deregulation must include and be exemplified by a smaller yet more efficient central government.

Deregulation and State reform

The growing concern about ownership and the transfer of public enterprises to the private sector, to civil corporations or to local organizations is another unavoidable aspect of a policy of internal deregulation, the liberalization of foreign trade and economic and political pluralism.

Ownership rights

It would be both difficult and premature to attempt an evaluation of the results of structural reform in Latin America. First, because such reforms were initiated only a very few years ago. Second, because not all of the countries have undertaken them. Third, because the pace, emphasis and results of the reforms vary. Nevertheless, for the time being, a number of questions need to be answered.

The first question could be elucidation of the degree of consensus among the financial institutions in Washington concerning specific solutions to the problems of given countries. Many Latin American economic experts assert, whether explicitly or implicitly, that what is needed to restructure their economies and revitalize growth, especially from a political viewpoint, is a national consensus rather than one imported from abroad. In fact, many Latin American governments instituted these reforms in response to their own needs and past experiences. On the one hand, as mentioned above, the countries of the region began to repudiate the import substitution strategy about twenty years ago, on the basis of both conceptual considerations and the evaluation of their results. On the other hand, in these same circles, there is an obvious trend toward forms of economic thinking more inclined toward internal deregulation of the economies, their opening to the exterior and the promotion of exports. The Washington community, meanwhile, is no longer interested solely in promoting adjustment policies aimed at stabilizing and normalizing the balance of payments position, but is also proposing reforms designed to create a climate more favorable to economic growth, the pursuit of equity, the revaluation of development theory and even the State's role in this process.

Other vital topics

In this connection, Washington's agenda is expanding to include such vital concerns as social equity, protection of the environment, the fight against drug trafficking, defending human rights and promoting democracy. It would be contradictory, then, if the economic reforms proposed to the Latin American countries made it difficult to achieve goals such as those mentioned above.

The new economic debate in Latin America

I have already noted how concern about economic growth—or development—which was so strong among the classical economists, was eclipsed in this century, a situation that continued until the end of the Second World War. This conflict marked the demise of colonialism and the entrance of the world's least developed regions onto the international stage. Some economists of the period began observing that the economies of the underdeveloped countries had characteristics very different from those of the more advanced countries. The most striking of these differences stemmed from their close economic, political and cultural ties to some of the developed countries, to which they exported the raw materials they specialized in and from which they imported manufactures, capital goods, technology, investments, institutions, ideas and the values upon which their development processes were based. The fledgling industries of the least developed countries were characterized by extreme structural heterogeneity and were divided into sectors of different size, productivity and capacity to absorb the work force, with very few linkages between them.

With the exception of export activities and the urban sector, there were practically no markets for goods and services since most of the economic activity and the majority of the active population were concentrated in very backward rural endeavors. There were very few modern capitalist enterprises; most were involved in the export sector and relied on foreign capital, with few venturing into the manufacturing sector. The physical infrastructure was very precarious and was designed primarily to serve the export sectors and urban areas, while social services—health and education—were also limited to the cities. There were not many banking institutions and the ones that did exist were weak and predominantly foreign; due to the imbalance and lack of intersectoral integration of the underdeveloped economies, there were almost no financial markets. As already mentioned, because of these same characteristics, the commodity and factor markets were very far from functioning smoothly. The State was institutionally weak and politically uninvolved, barely concerned about development problems, and had virtually no presence in rural areas. The scholarly Latin Americans who began to write in the postwar period, such as Raúl Prebisch and the economists who participated in his work and ideas—Celso Furtado, Victor Urquidi and many others—along with social analysts of the stature of José Medina Echavarría, made extremely important contributions to the analysis of the social and economic structures of their countries.

The difficulties they had in explaining the functioning of these economies from the viewpoint of neoclassical thinking, whether marginalist or Keynesian, with its emphasis on markets and the price system as the determinants of short-term economic performance, led them to seek an interpretation of the structure of the Latin American economies founded on their historical evolution and a careful study of the various national realities.

Emergence of the structuralist school

These analyses led to the structuralist view of the development process referred to above. As is well known, this name was conferred in a dispute between these analysts and traditional economists about the causes and possible remedies of inflation, an endemic problem in the Latin American economies, which the traditionalists tried to explain and to attack from a purely monetary perspective, ignoring the structural origins of the process. Other Latin American analysts believed that the markets and the price system were unable to function properly in these economies because of a series of structural distortions or bottlenecks, which included, first, a kind of productive specialization and a form of commercial integration with the large industrial centers that caused the terms of trade to evolve consistently in a manner contrary to the interests of these countries, forcing them to transfer to such centers a large part of the surplus generated by their productive activities; the lack of international or domestic financial markets, which further restricted the investment capabilities of these countries, thus reinforcing the limitations created by the poor purchasing power of their exports; the predominance of a vulnerable, disjointed and extremely diverse economic structure, which tended to concentrate technical advances and income and was incapable of productively absorbing the increase in the labor force; and the need for various forms of State intervention to correct these distortions, given the market's inability to do so.

Three distinct aspects

The structuralists departed from the traditional view, which held that development was powered by capital accumulation and the creation of full employment guided by the market, in three basic areas.

For them, and from a macroeconomic point of view, the main component of the accumulation process was not domestic savings but foreign resources, which, because of the form of international economic integration of these countries and the trend toward the deterioration of their terms of trade, would always be insufficient to enable them to import the goods needed for their development. The reallocation of resources to the import sector was not a solution due to the inelasticity of demand caused by the price of such goods and the buyers' incomes. Therefore, it was not possible to count on obtaining the resources needed to import industrial goods through foreign trade, and it was preferable to develop a domestic manufacturing sector to replace such imports. Moreover, it was believed that the manufacturing sector was the standard bearer of technical progress, which could be disseminated from that sector to the rest of the economy. Naturally, under the existing circumstances, this process could not move forward in an environment of heavy competition without a reasonable degree of protection. The objective of the commercial policy of these countries was not to correct their balance of payments but to restructure relative prices in favor of the industrial sector—to the detriment of agriculture—by means of monetary, tariff or fiscal measures of a preferential nature.

Second, at the microeconomic level, structuralism pointed up the flaws and the lack of continuity in the Latin American economies. One major problem was the slow progress of agriculture, attributed primarily to the prevalence of outmoded landholding systems. The lack of intersectoral integration of the productive system and, consequently, of positive forward and backward linkages between the various productive activities was also criticized. This lack of integration also lowered the incentive to invest and to organize true capital markets in these countries. The shortcomings of the physical and social infrastructure and the geographic imbalances of the economic activities constituted additional barriers to the normal functioning of the markets.

The macro and microeconomic conditions mentioned above pointed to the need for a strong presence of the State in the economy to overcome them, an outlook which differed from that of the neoclassicists who, in this regard, remained faithful to Adam Smith and the other founders of economic thought. It was believed that development was a consequence of the implementation of effective public policies and not a natural evolution of market forces or of free competition. The State's action was supposed to correct the deficiencies in the market through planning, as well as contributing directly to capital formation through expansion of the infrastructure, the financing of large industrial projects and the operation of public enterprises.

The structuralist view was translated into policy proposals. The orientation toward the domestic market and the replacement of imports were the key components of these policies. There was great distrust of the foreign market and of primary exports. Import substitution seemed much more appropriate than the traditional strategy, which was oriented toward foreign markets and benefited the agricultural sector. Nevertheless, as already pointed out, the new strategy soon encountered limitations, failed to overcome the external financial vulnerability of the Latin American economies, created sectoral imbalances, and unleashed inflationary and fiscal pressures.

After a time, criticism of structuralism, which had started at the very outset, began to intensify. In the 1960s, structuralist pro-

Its influence on economic policies

grams benefited from injections of capital from the Alliance for Progress, but the latter's influence soon waned, further exposing the weaknesses of this strategy. Because of its reformist approach, its redistributive content and its State-oriented character, structuralism and its strategies were opposed from the beginning by conservatives, who favored more traditional policies and the reduction of the size and role of the State. Structuralist strategies also drew attacks from radical political groups, who wanted more sweeping, revolutionary measures and who expressed their views through the dependency theory. But it was the conservative critics who finally gained the upper hand and imposed their views. In the mid-1960s, in both Brazil and Argentina, the civilian governments were replaced by military regimes committed to more traditional economic policies and ending inflation. Circumstances again challenged the structuralist school when the oil crisis erupted in 1973-1974 and it became necessary to implement adjustment policies conditioned by a process of heavy foreign borrowing, made possible by conditions in the international financial markets in the midst of an unstable, recessionary world economic environment. The crisis in 1982 caused by servicing the external debt again made it necessary to try new policies.

The obsolescence of the import substitution model and the subsequent debt crisis made it impractical to continue as before. To become integrated in the world economy, the Latin American countries had to reestablish macroeconomic stability and productive competitiveness. They had to ensure fiscal equilibria, correct exchange rates, positive interest rates that would not subsidize capital-intensive import substitution industries, real wages determined by international competition, and substantially curtailed State intervention. The experience of the Southeast Asian countries in the preceding twenty years was especially relevant to this development strategy.

Thus, the stabilization and adjustment policies the countries of the region had to implement to deal with the crisis were generating experiences of a different nature, which the structuralist camp began to analyze critically. The perceptions of the realities of the region, together with the lessons learned from the collapse of the planned economy system and the experience of the economies of Southeast Asia, began to be analyzed in light of the structuralist view of the Latin American economy.

There is a marked revisionism in Latin American thought concerning not only the past but also certain basic perspectives of the original Latin American consensus. These revisionist tendencies hold that the basic limitations of Latin American development, identified by the structuralist school, are still present; namely, the existence of an inadequate pattern of external integration, the predominance of a disparate productive structure, and the persistence of inequitable income distribution. Other structural aspects remain that affect the functioning of the Latin American economies more than the rules of the market. These include the type of foreign trade the countries specialize in, the degree of market concentration, the intensity and orientation of forward and backward productive linkages, control of the means of production by various sectors (e.g. the State, the private sector and transnational capital), the landholding system, the pattern of income distribution, the functioning of the financial markets and the degree of incorporation of advanced technology, together with sociological and political factors related to the level of labor organization, the class structure and the political system.[34]

Nevertheless, more than the predominance of the neoclassicist or the neostructuralist view, what stands out in the economic thinking of Latin America and in the economic policies of the respective governments is a trend toward agreement about certain specific points which, on the one hand, depart from the traditional view of Latin American development prevalent in the postwar era and, on the other, tend to correct the excesses of the neoliberal policies applied in the most severe phase of the adjustment period.

The trend toward consensus

Included among these points are, first, concern about the size and the effects of the transfer of resources abroad to service the debt. On the one hand, this massive transfer of resources threatens stabilization, which is one of the main objectives of these policies, and on the other, occurs at the expense of the resources available for investment, thus jeopardizing the development process in both the short and the long term.

Five points of convergence

Second, this incipient merger of ideas gives new importance to—and views from a new perspective—the old problem of inflation, in contrast to the relatively superficial responses of the monetarist school and the complacency regarding this phenomenon exhibited by the old structuralists. The new consensus not only assigns the highest priority to stabilization but also recognizes the fact that inflation is caused by incompatible pressures on the factors of production and can be corrected only insofar as a firm income policy is formulated, which could include specific ways of controlling prices and/or wages and, in general, explicitly negotiated social compacts that tend to alleviate these pressures.

---

[34] See O. Sunkel, *El desarrollo desde dentro: un enfoque neoestructuralista para América Latina*, Mexico, Fondo de Cultura Económica, 1992.

Third, there is also agreement on a more pressing concern having to do with the distribution of income and the need to attack the problem of extreme poverty using the scarce resources available, within the context of clearer consensual policy decisions, more imaginative solutions and more sharply-focused programs.

Fourth, the emerging view unanimously stresses the importance of trade liberalization and the entry of the Latin American economies in the international arena. This transformation requires a more active, more selective and better-oriented integration by endogenous forces and institutions to allay the undesirable effects of trade liberalization on our economies and to enable them to create dynamic advantages through conscious support for the most promising activities and integration in the appropriate markets.

Finally, there is also a more consensual and less ideological view of the State's role, which is in need of major reform, although the orientation and extent of such a reform are still not clear. In this regard, it seems to be generally agreed that the market must be supported by selective action on the part of the State, which, in addition to its usual functions (having to do with maintaining macroeconomic balances, social equity and the provision of public services), includes the promotion or stimulation of missing markets (such as long-term capital markets), the strengthening of incomplete markets (such as the technological market), the correction of structural distortions (such as the disparateness of the productive structure), the concentration of ownership and income or the fragmentation of the capital and labor markets, and the elimination or overcoming of limitations to growth caused by insufficient returns to scale, learning processes or externalities.

In any case, it appears that no one today seriously thinks that the Latin American economies should resume looking only inward to support growth or that they should again become deeply pessimistic about foreign markets, negligently manage short-term macroeconomic policy, be complacent about overall imbalances, or advocate excessive State intervention with large public outlays.

The quiet transformation of Latin America

In fact, as is true of every major crisis, all was not lost in this process. Just as the recovery of the world economy was made possible by the destruction caused by the war, so can the Latin American economies be revitalized after the havoc caused by indebtedness and the adjustment process, which can be considered the "moral equivalents of war." What did we gain in the lost decade? The magnitude of the crisis and its painful costs tend to make us forget that we also learned important lessons and even made some progress as a result of a kind of quiet revolution. As I see it, these lessons constitute Latin America's greatest asset in solving its problems or unresolved challenges. Of these, I would like to point out the following:

A learning process

To begin with, I should mention a benefit of great importance: the return of democracy to most of our countries. This fact cannot be undervalued because of setbacks in the economic order. The advances in the restoration of democratic institutions, the practice of political consensus or agreement and the defense of human rights constitute an attainment of historic importance, especially since it occurred in the restrictive environment of the crisis. In light of the recent past, the restitution of democracy conveys three important messages: first, the humanist tradition and social maturity of the Latin American countries ultimately demonstrated that the establishment of exceptional regimes is not the only possible response in periods of transition and unrest; second, in many cases, the notion that stability and economic growth can be achieved by only authoritarian systems of government was also disproved; and, third, it has become much clearer that economic, technological and social modernization can only be effected rapidly and enduringly in a climate of respect for freedoms, social participation and the integration of all sectors. But perhaps the most outstanding characteristic of the new Latin American political climate is the tendency to seek consensus and agreement, which is, moreover, in keeping with the current style of world politics.[35]

Restoration of democracy

On this plane, the first achievement has been the establishment of stabilization programs to deal with inflationary processes that, in many cases, bordered on hyperinflation. The region can now point to some of the most notable cases of combating runaway inflation, such as the experiences of Bolivia, Costa Rica and Chile, and, more recently, Ecuador, Mexico and Venezuela. The drop in inflation rates in recent years is a clear demonstration of the positive results of the current policies. Argentina, Peru and Nicaragua provide further evidence of this trend. Debt reduction programs, because of

The search for stability

---

[35] See D.J. Dionne, Jr., *Why Americans Hate Politics*, New York, Simon and Schuster, 1991.

their significant impact on fiscal accounts, have played an important role in the success of these policies.

Along with stabilization programs, nearly all of the countries have initiated strict fiscal adjustment programs. Latin America now recognizes that the subject of fiscal deficits is at the center of the major macroeconomic disequilibria it has experienced in the past and that unless it is addressed decisively and courageously, it will be extremely difficult to establish a minimum degree of stability upon which sound, self-sustaining development processes can be based. The region as a whole is now moving toward greater macroeconomic balance, which is not always easy and, moreover, has high political and social costs. The change is a clear manifestation of the determination to combat one of the factors that contributes most to perpetuating injustice in Latin American societies today: the prevalence of high inflation rates. The people of Latin America now understand very clearly that the most damaging tax on the lower classes is high inflation, and, therefore, that the social cost of implementing stabilization programs is far less than the persistent costs that have fallen on these social groups in recent years as a result of inflationary disequilibria. Hence, we have witnessed the political courage and even the unprecedented degree of social tolerance that have supported many of these programs in the recent experience of Latin America.

International openness

A third aspect of this quiet transformation is the growing openness of Latin America to foreign trade. It is now acknowledged that in an increasingly interdependent world characterized by the emergence of a global economy, if vigorous economic development is to be achieved, there is no alternative to ever more competitive participation in the international economy. This concept has been absorbed and assimilated by the people of Latin America and is now a generally-held conviction. There is no economic development in isolation and, consequently, the countries must become in tune with the world economy by increasing their international competitiveness. To achieve this position, unprecedented trade liberalization, tariff reduction and export promotion programs have been launched throughout Latin America. The lowering of the levels of protection in Latin America places it on par with the economies of the industrialized countries; in some cases, this change was achieved with a rapidity and a thoroughness unknown in international experience. All of this points to the acceleration of a process leading to the creation of economies that are much more competitive than they were in the past. Nevertheless, the persistence of recessionary trends in the world economy and the danger that the current protectionist trends will continue to pose, raise doubts about how these efforts will be received by the international community. This uncertainty reveals a potential lack of symmetry between its response and the efforts that the Latin American countries have made to open their economies.

A fourth area of this transformation process in which advances have been made is the reorganization of the State and the objective of greater efficiency in the performance of its functions, as well as the growing trend toward the limitation of such functions to a smaller number of centralized activities. The kind of involvement it had in the past in innumerable economic activities is now being ruled out. This tendency has led to an intensification throughout Latin America of the search for greater efficiency in the public sector in general, especially public enterprises, and to the initiation of a series of privatization processes and other decentralization efforts by the State. State reform is now not only an important element in terms of deepening the democratization process at all levels but also an essential condition for increasing the economic efficiency of our countries. As explained below, modernization of the State is a key component of the productive reorganization and the international integration of our countries.[36]

Modification of the State's role

These mainstays of the adjustment policies and structural reforms were accompanied by programs designed to solve the debt problem, which, once the initial concern about protecting the creditor bank's position was allayed, were oriented toward alleviating the burden on the debtor countries. This shift occurred under the Brady Plan and, more recently, the Enterprise for the Americas Initiative, which allowed some of these countries to turn away from their deep concern about external indebtedness that prevailed in the eighties. As mentioned above, this change does not mean that the subject is no longer important or that it is not still a serious concern for some countries.

Managing the external debt

There have also been some intangible advances, which represent additional lessons learned from the crisis. Those of us who have worked in Latin America for many years know that progress which is not reflected in the statistics has been made in the region. In many cases, this progress has consisted of changes in attitude, in the forms of social, governmental or business organization, or in the

Some intangible advances

---

[36] See R. Wade, *Governing the Market, Economic Theory and the Role of Government*, Princeton University Press, 1990, and F. Larrain and M. Selowski, *The Public Sector and the Latin American Crisis*, San Francisco, ICS Press, 1991.

lessons that the development experience has provided in recent decades. The first of these lessons is the one apparently learned by most of our political leaders, who are now more wary of populist options and who are committed to more prudent policies aimed at maintaining overall balances. Beyond these circles, the region's economic leaders generally understand the necessity of making the adjustment and more efficiently utilizing economic resources, both human and capital, thereby increasing the competitiveness of their countries. We have also learned that runaway inflation is socially costly and difficult, which reinforces the objective of achieving economic stability as a condition for making the adjustment and subsequently instituting policies aimed at economic growth in a stable environment. Similarly, we have learned that without adjustment, social problems can become insoluble and more devastating. But we have also learned that there is a limit to how much society will tolerate and that adjustment programs must therefore be accompanied by emergency social compensation measures and a clear vision of a different future for disadvantaged social groups.

Another lesson concerns the need to give priority to market mechanisms when State intervention in economic processes becomes excessive, as it did in recent decades; this change involves a gradual process of market deregulation, which will promote efficiency in the use of resources by both the public and the private sectors. A complementary lesson indicates that State reform is necessary in Latin America to eliminate its chronic deficits, increase its efficiency and advance the privatization of public enterprises and the decentralization of State functions; this type of reform does not imply, however, that the State will disappear or be weakened. We are also beginning to understand that the pressing social needs that have been accumulating in the region must be attended to gradually, that the modernization of our economies and the revitalization of growth are essential conditions for attending to these needs, and that even now it is possible to begin doing so by reorienting and sharpening the focus of social spending. Another lesson is that the expansion and diversification of exports and, consequently, the liberalization of foreign trade and the opening of the economies constitute a key factor for managing the debt problem and furthering the economic transition.

The results of this quiet transformation of Latin America are already appearing on several levels:

Early results

a)   The growth rate has improved. The Bank's most recent reports indicate that in 1991 the GDP of the region as a whole had grown approximately 3 percent, in contrast to a decrease of nearly 1 percent in 1990;

b)   Inflation has abated in most countries, although it is still high in others, which, consequently, are in the initial stages of the process. According to ECLAC, inflation indexes, which had hovered around 1,200 percent in 1989 and 1990, dropped to 300 percent per annum in 1991 and show promising signs for the future; and

c)   Capital is again flowing to the region. The repatriation of Latin American capital has been remarkably energized, strong incentives have been created for foreign investments and the securities markets in most of the countries have been revitalized. According to the latest report of the OECD, in 1991 the region experienced a positive transfer of resources for the first time since 1983. As indicated above, between 1983 and 1990, negative transfers abroad were around $20 billion a year. In 1991 this transfer turned positive, representing a resource flow of approximately $15 billion .

All of these numbers are important indicators of the early results of the quiet revolution mentioned above.

Toward a Latin American economic consensus

There are undoubtedly wide areas of agreement between the world's major financial centers and Latin America about how to reignite the development process at this stage, including certain principal points and basic objectives as well as numerous policies and specific measures. Nevertheless, there are also differences in emphasis and, in many instances, differences of perception.

A new development discipline

It is only natural, after so many years of making adjustments and struggling to achieve stability, that the renewal of development and the raising of living standards should be given special priority. To achieve these objectives, the restoration of macroeconomic balances is essential but not sufficient, just as basing the development effort on a series of standard, preconceived notions would be inadequate.

Latin America needs, above all, to make an enormous internal effort focused not only on development but also on the quality of such development, in order to solve the problems of equity and to address the problems of poverty.

To achieve these goals, with all the uncertainties, surprises, successes and failures of any such process, the region must analyze its own vision and its own internal discipline before resolutely undertaking the fascinating task of economic and social development.

It is toward this objective that the quiet transformation in Latin America is moving, in harmony with similar changes taking place throughout the world. Nevertheless, some questions that are worth reconsidering remain. In Latin America, have we discovered a definitive formula that will put an end to economic stagnation and allow us to look forward to a future of sustained development? To what extent will our economic reforms be sufficient to ensure positive results in this direction?

Regarding the first question, both economic history and developmental experience prove that there are no magic formulas or absolute models for orienting these processes. One of the factors that has most compromised the political and economic growth of the Latin American countries is the tendency to attribute a kind of ideological intangibility to policies that seem appropriate at a given moment. Any policy is, by definition, a response to a given set of circumstances. Only the adherents of historic materialism or the most extreme liberalism could have thought themselves capable of predicting or putting an end to history. History changes constantly and unceasingly, creating different experiences and giving rise to various stages and situations that require appropriate responses. Consequently, I do not believe that there is any one, absolute formula for addressing the problems of Latin America and the world.

Regarding the effectiveness of the proposed measures, I would venture to say that the economic reforms currently underway, which are the fruit of recent years' experience, are a necessary component which, in and of themselves, are not sufficient to ensure a pattern of development that responds to our historic experience and our social and political life. Hence, in addition to supporting these reforms, which are aimed at economic efficiency, other measures related to the political situation, the social conditions and the institutional structure of the Latin American countries must also be implemented. This path will not be easy and, therefore, a number of concerns about Latin America's future remain.

If some of the major concerns from the Latin American perspective were to be singled out, mention would have to be made, first of all, of the need to recognize the differences that exist between the economies of the region in terms of their size, productive structure, form of external integration and socio-political systems. These differences explain the various reactions to similar reforms occurring in the countries of the region. Liberalism postulated that rational calculation and freedom of choice are essential characteristics of the economic agents operating in markets free of any distortion. Structuralism made an important contribution to economic analysis by hypothesizing that the behavior of such agents is determined by a set of behavioral principles imposed by the historical, socio-economic and institutional contexts in which they operate. The greater or lesser degree of resistance the structural reforms have encountered in the various countries in which they have been introduced, and the greatly differing results produced by each of them, are largely explained by these differences. Hence, we see the danger of making too many generalizations.

Another concern is the pace and sequencing of these reforms in light of each individual case. The industrialized countries' own experience indicates that reforms cannot always be implemented quickly; they must proceed in stages. Marcelo Selowsky has proposed a plan for this process: the first stage would focus on curbing inflation and reducing fiscal deficits; the second on establishing a system of incentives and reforming the public sector, including efforts to increase competitiveness through deregulation; and the third stage would seek to revitalize growth by increasing the level of investment.

An additional concern relates to what has been said about maintaining macroeconomic balances as a necessary but insufficient condition for promoting development. The essential elements in this regard are a thorough industrial reorganization and true economic competitiveness. There is no guarantee that economic stability will automatically lead to the necessary reforms. Such reforms require a vision and a conscious effort. This effort must not be oriented preferentially to the domestic market, as it was in the early stages of Latin American development, but rather to international markets, taking into account the changes that have occurred in this regard both within and outside the region. The State must be modernized in order to meet this challenge. The lack of confidence in the market that prevailed in the early decades of the Latin American experience must be overcome in order to assign a preponderant role to business and the private sector, duly integrated in a full network of connections between their labor base, the educational system, the technological infrastructure, the financial system, the public and private institutional apparatus and the international markets.

There is also concern about the danger of neglecting pressing social problems, especially extreme poverty, unemployment, social security systems and, above all, the education of the young. The quality of education and the development of the human resources needed to effect the essential productive transformations must be a cause for concern in our countries.

Finally, I would like to emphasize Latin America's concern with foreign relations. I am not going to insist here on the need for improvements in the international economic environment and in cooperative programs for development, because I plan to do so later, but they are essential conditions for supporting the economic reforms currently underway in Latin America. I would like to stress the need for Latin America to open its markets to the world and, in so doing, to cultivate its special historic relationship with the United States and Europe, as well as with Asia and other developing countries. Greater political and economic ties with the rest of the world will have the positive effect of "anchoring" our development strategies, as occurred with the countries that more recently joined the European Community, and achieved greater stability because of their association with major economic and world political centers. Latin America's development options are to be found not in isolation but rather in its integration with the rest of the world.

I would like to add to these concerns three comments, which may help to clear up some of the confusion we sometimes feel in this transitional stage.

Comments on the current discussion

First, what is at issue in the current discussion of Latin America's alternatives are not conflicting economic theories or development models but rather an up-to-date reading of the new political and economic circumstances our countries are facing vis-à-vis an interpretation based on diagnoses of past situations. What is at issue, in other words, is not the absolute truth of our cherished ideas about development but rather to what extent these ideas reflect the new characteristics and, therefore, the new challenges.

Second, although as always in the history of Latin American development there is now a discrepancy between the ideas and interests of the industrialized countries and our own, what stands out is not the difference of opinion but the growing margin of consensus that could be identified both within the region and between it and the international community if the region were to complete its "productive transformation with equity" and reinforce its processes of integration to negotiate with the industrialized world from more mature positions based on shared interests.

Third, an interpretation of the new circumstances implies adapting many of the basic development objectives pursued in the postwar era to these same circumstances. Thus, what at one time might have been accomplished through industrialization must now be achieved through the productive transformation of Latin America by means of a comprehensive modernization process in which protection must be reconciled with the objectives of greater international competitiveness. Interdependence with the international economy must be managed on the basis of profits derived from competitive integration within Latin America and between the region and the rest of the world, thereby developing comparative advantages. The State's action is still essential, but it must support rather than stifle the action of the private agents. This role implies more selective and efficient State involvement, including the establishment of rules favoring market forces, the strengthening of its regulatory capacity, the acceptance of its primary responsibility for social policies and the search for sustainable environmental development.

In fact, longstanding Latin American development objectives, as yet unfulfilled, must be adapted to the new conditions. And to identify them, new institutions are needed. Perhaps the most important message conveyed by this latter comment is that the greatest task confronting the countries of the region is that of effecting a thorough institutional overhaul, encompassing not only a reform of the State and greater interaction between it and the market, but also the strengthening of agents such as civil corporations, small businesses and the informal sector, regional and local communities, and the participation of women and young people in development, primarily through educational reform. Nearly twenty years ago Paul Streeten stressed the importance of the administrative skills "that determine the ability to change production structures through public policies as well as the time needed to do so" and added that "the political structure and the interests and loyalties of the governing groups determine what actions are possible and in which cases sociological and political restrictions apply."[37]

---

[37] P. Streeten, "Comments," in H. Hughes, ed., *Prospects for Partnership: Industrialization and Trade Policies in the 1970s.* Baltimore, Johns Hopkins University Press, 1973.

The productive transformation of Latin America

Chapter IV

Some lessons of the 1980s

We have learned lessons from the experiences and debates that I have recounted in the opening chapters of this book and from the changes that have taken place in the international economy. In the first place, achieving stability and re-establishing macroeconomic equilibria are essential if Latin American countries are to embark once again on the path toward economic development and insert themselves more vigorously into world markets. Furthermore, the countries' increased dexterity and prudence in managing their national economies are the product of the significant and painful experiences of the past decade. This is not enough, however, for it is still possible to distinguish not only between Latin American countries that have rigorously and intensely applied these policies and those that have not, but between those that, having applied these policies, have boosted their economic growth and their exports and those that have not. Something more than just re-establishing equilibria is needed.

Stability with development

The mounting problems that beset Latin America during the postwar development process, particularly as a result of the critical 1980s, are not related solely to macroeconomics. They also include the drop in interest rates, the obsolescence of the region's industrial base and physical infrastructure, the failure to keep up with worldwide technological innovation, the disruption of sectoral linkages within the economies, the misuse of natural resources, the drastic contraction in the countries' financial capacity, and the deterioration of public institutions and their linkages with the private sector. The 1980s, however, did not only teach the region to manage macroeconomic policy more rigorously; through the silent transformation of Latin America's economies, it provided new directions and laid the groundwork for productive restructuring and the countries' reinsertion into the international markets—processes that will permit their economies to resume the growth required to overcome some of the

Some structural factors

region's problems. First of all, I would like to discuss the more general changes that have occurred in this respect.

Interaction between policy and the economy

We have affirmed that, on the political level, the past decade should be recalled as a period of significant democratization. Paradoxically, this process has unfolded in the midst of the worst possible economic conditions. It is reasonable to assume that forging political systems that are participatory, open, and stable is easier in a climate of burgeoning economic growth and relatively high levels of social welfare levels. The circumstances surrounding the re-establishment or bolstering of democracy in Latin America could not have been further from this scenario. I believe that the sober acceptance of democratic institutions by the mass of the people in our societies is grounded in the painful acknowledgement of past errors and, hence, in the suffering and maturing of both the citizenry and its leaders. The difficulties created by the excessive ideological factionalism often present in our Latin American political systems and government failure to reconcile political objectives with the goals of economic growth opened the door in many cases to authoritarian regimes that either did not solve the countries' problems, or did so only in part, at the cost of sacrificing basic liberties and the working class.

Thus, the trend toward realism and ideological moderation, together with the search for rapprochement and agreement, is beginning to gain ground as a new style of political action. This approach also involves a better understanding of the relationship between economics and political life: today, more than ever, we acknowledge the presence of economic constraints on the workings of democracy and of the parameters of political and social tolerance within which economic processes can function. This recognition, and the growing complexity of Latin America's economies and societies, have moved the majority of the region's governments to employ an ever-broader and homogeneous set of elements to technify their activities.

Social transformations

Nowhere has the impact of the lost decade been more painfully felt than in the social sector. The decline in income and real wages among the lower classes and the rise in poverty, unemployment, and economic exclusion have been the worst aspects of this decade. Nevertheless, this difficult process has also left behind some lessons and contributions. The groups most adversely affected have often reacted in self-defense, creating self-help ventures at the community or grassroots level. Growing confidence in market mechanisms has helped eliminate some types of state intervention, regulations, or subsidies in a way that, while sometimes overdone, has strengthened the role of free enterprise and the private sector, stimulating creativity and competition among economic players. For example, some of the processes of privatization and decentralization generated by the adjustment policies and the revised role of the State have produced these same results.

The weakening of traditional economic institutions and sectors and the emergence of new activities within a climate of greater competitiveness have accentuated the changes that were beginning to take place in the composition of the work force, making it more flexible and diversified. The traditionally sharp distinctions between rural and urban workers, salaried industrial employees and marginal workers in the urban sector, and blue and white collar workers, have grown fuzzy, giving way to a gradual and nuanced social and occupational structure. However, these changes were also substantially due to the emergence of a vast informal sector of self-employed workers, still lacking access to the markets, credit and to the institutional organization and services required to enhance their training, productivity, and income. In any case, though burdened by great disequilibria and inequalities, there was a proliferation of public and private players with very different purviews and functions across the entire social spectrum, plus a growing interaction among them. The danger of alienation between leaders and the people at the grassroots level, the lack of representativeness in government agencies, and the accompanying tendency toward greater technification of the political process, might find a certain degree of compensation in the strengthening of the various social agents mentioned above.

On the economic level, despite the significant retreats suffered during the long period of adjustment and debt servicing, the need to maintain macroeconomic equilibria has been recognized. In several cases, a promising productive restructuring has begun, partly as a result of deliberate policies and partly due to the silent transformation brought about by the situation in Latin America. Finally, the external openness of these countries has increased, and exports have expanded. Similarly, the artificial dilemmas of the past concerning industry versus agriculture, the domestic versus the international market, planning versus market forces, government versus private enterprise, and the sectoral versus systemic nature of these reforms have been resolved to a great extent.

The beginning of economic reconstruction

On the regional level, there has been progress toward new forms of concerted action among diverse groups of Latin American countries—action sanctioned at the highest political levels—and within less cumbersome formulas. The governments have reached new integration agreements, bilateral or multilateral, that are not only more focused, but much more oriented toward complementation of the productive sectors of the countries involved, greater competitive-

Concerted action on a regional scale

ness, and the furthering of the countries' insertion into the international markets.

On the international level, as I have already noted, despite an extremely restrictive external environment in trade and finance, the countries of the region have developed a more positive attitude toward the international markets and their own potential for gradually and selectively penetrating them through a deliberate effort at productive restructuring. To varying degrees, nearly every country has instituted processes to further external openness, increase international competitiveness, and expand exports. Unfortunately, as I mentioned in the previous section, the sharp contradiction between efforts by the majority of Latin American countries to apply these policies, which have been strongly recommended by the international community, and the latter's failure to recognize such efforts in certain key areas is noteworthy. Thus, for example, negotiations and programs aimed at liberalizing world trade and establishing satisfactory flows of international financing have been insufficient or have stalled. Meanwhile, economic coordination in a multipolar world relies solely on informal and direct mechanisms for policy coordination among the world's major economies, as in the case of the Group of Seven, without the broad multilateral mechanisms that reflect conditions created by the degree of global economic interdependence.

The challenge of productive restructuring

Together with learning the decisive lessons necessary to meet these basic conditions, Latin American countries have come to even more general and important conclusions: that future growth will be ever more dependent on the incorporation of technological know-how and innovation into the production process; that it is not enough for this growth to occur only in some sectors, but rather, it must be an integral process; and that it cannot rely solely on the absorption of external models or resources, but must possess a dynamic that is primarily endogenous in nature.[38] This does not mean that growth cannot be

---

[38] ECLAC argued very persuasively in favor of this approach in its report *Transformación productiva con equidad*, Santiago, Chile, 1990. The late Fernando Fajnzylber did also, both inside and outside the agency, through *La industrialización trunca de América Latina*, Mexico, Nueva Imagen, 1982, and *De la caja negra al casillero vacío*, ECLAC, 1990.

unbalanced and still benefit from the transmission of the dynamic effects brought about by modernity and development. It does mean, however, that the attitudes of the economic players and the structure of the economies should be strongly oriented toward promoting flexibility, intersectoral linkage, and the conditions for diffusing technological innovation throughout the economy. This leads to the need to revise some of the prevailing notions of the past, to be more concerned about the quality of investments, and to understand that development cannot come about simply by adopting a correct price system or applying a series of isolated sectoral policies.

As is well known, several of the structural characteristics of Latin American countries have militated against a productive restructuring aimed at increasing their international competitiveness and based on the absorption and diffusion of technological change and the intersectoral integration of their economies. Among these characteristics are the asymmetry with which these countries have inserted themselves into the international economy through exports of raw materials, with little structural competitiveness; the consequent external financial gap; the weakness of direct foreign investment; insufficient domestic savings, due in part to the vicious circle of poverty and in part to an unsatisfactory pattern of consumption; the inability to absorb technological innovation; the progressive paralysis of public institutions, together with a lack of vigor in the private sector—not to mention resistance to change on the part of certain interest groups; the economy's inability to productively absorb the new work force; and a disjointed pattern of industrialization, inadequately supported by the countries' own endowment of natural resources.

Historical barriers to restructuring

The transformations in the world economy and in the productive structure of Latin American countries are exerting pressure to remove these obstacles. At the same time, in some cases these same forces are creating the need to redefine the strategies to overcome them. Such is the case, for example, regarding the role of direct foreign investment, the productive potential of the work force employed in the informal or service sectors, and development based on traditional natural resources vis-à-vis the expansion and diversification of exports deriving from the development and transformation of other resources.

Therefore, it is becoming widely accepted that the resumption of growth in Latin America will depend on a productive restructuring aimed at increasing the region's international competitiveness through the incorporation and spread of technological change. Michael Porter offers several alternative explanations for the origins of

Roots of international competitiveness

countries' international competitiveness.[39] Some believe that it is a macroeconomic phenomenon, generated by the proper management of exchange rates, interest rates, and fiscal deficits, even though there are countries that have enjoyed rapid economic growth while maintaining fiscal deficits (Japan), overvalued currencies (Germany), or high interest rates (Italy). Others assert that competitiveness depends on an abundant supply of cheap labor, the experiences of Germany, Sweden, and Switzerland notwithstanding. Still others believe that competitiveness is linked to abundant natural resources, which has not been the case in recent decades for the countries with the most dynamic economies, such as Germany, Japan, or Italy, nor for the most developed regions within some countries.[40] It has recently been argued that competitiveness is generally associated with deliberate government policies to promote certain sectors. However, there is evidence that this correlation is not perfect, as in the case of Japan, where the production of fax machines, copiers, robots, and new materials has received little government support, while policies to bolster certain areas, such as aeronautics, have met with minimal success.

Nevertheless, despite numerous examples of this type, experience indicates that competitiveness is closely tied to maintaining policies that effectively promote innovation throughout the economy. From an opposing viewpoint, there are those who claim that competitiveness derives from adequate organizational and managerial capacity at the entrepreneurial level. Without a doubt, this is an important element, though it should be borne in mind that no single formula exists in these areas and that each country and each activity may require its own peculiar kind of organization and managerial style. It is not a matter of adopting certain successful organizational models, but rather, of developing a vigorous and systematic entrepreneurial response capability.

Ultimately, international competitiveness is the chief prerequisite that, given the current world economic situation, will allow the countries to improve their societies' welfare, and it depends chiefly on how productively each country makes use of its resources. The level of productivity, in turn, depends on the nature and quality

---

[39] M. E. Porter, *The Competitive Advantage of Nations*, New York, The Free Press, 1990.

[40] I have noted elsewhere Peter Drucker's observation on the tendency of the contemporary world economy to disassociate itself from its traditional sources of expansion, natural resources, and the work force.

of the goods and how efficiently they are produced—factors that determine their price in the market.

The matter becomes more complicated when one attempts to clarify what determines a nation's overall competitiveness, or even whether some nations are, on the whole, more competitive than others. A competitive country cannot be defined as one where every industrial area and every company is competitive, for in that case, no nation would fit the bill. A country is not competitive simply because it maintains a positive trade balance: Italy has exhibited chronic trade deficits, while Switzerland has kept its trade balance in equilibrium; both, nevertheless, have been highly competitive in world markets and have maintained an elevated standard of living. Similarly, it is not enough to be able to offer products at low prices in the international markets: Germany and Japan have long maintained very strong currencies and successfully exported at high prices, to the benefit of their societies' welfare. A country is not more competitive if its foreign trade generates more employment at depressed wages. True international competitiveness must be compatible with exporting quality products at reasonable prices and generating well-paying jobs.

Competitiveness at the national level

If a nation's international competitiveness depends on its economic productivity and this, in turn, determines its people's level of welfare, each country must attempt, as systemically as possible, to create the conditions necessary to raise the level of productivity of its industries and the firms that comprise them. This can be accomplished in ongoing activities by upgrading the quality of goods (diversifying them or adding new features) or raising efficiency levels. Comparative advantages can be developed in new sectors, permitting the transfer of labor once employed in older, less productive sectors. All this implies technological development, and success is usually reflected in the level of exports. Exports generated by a given branch of industry are a good indicator of its level of productivity, as is its ability to attract foreign investment. At the same time, the country can develop in areas where it is less efficient by investing in those activities abroad, or it can import the respective goods and services.

The general and the particular: a necessary consideration

In any case, what I wish to underscore is that a country's improvement in competitiveness is not a homogeneous process. Its successes are to be found somewhere between an overall and dictated approach to this problem at the national level, and efforts made or risks taken individually at the enterprise level. It is a process that essentially occurs in every branch of industry and its respective enterprises, but whose success presupposes an economic policy framework that favors innovation, greater productivity, and international competitiveness. It requires taking a much broader range of international economic factors into account, greater integration between the public and private sectors and the larger and smaller players who operate within each sector, and above all, progress toward a greater integration between the State, the scientific and technological community, and the productive financial sectors.

The search for this middle ground also assumes progress toward greater linkage within countries' productive systems. For historical reasons, integration between the various sectors of the economies has been extremely inadequate and has suffered from acute dichotomies: between the key primary exporting activity and the rest of the economy; between the industrial and agricultural sectors; between relatively modern branches of industry and others that have failed to move past the traditional stage; between directly productive activity and services; more recently, between the formal and informal sectors of the economy; and dating far back, between a broad spectrum of economic activities and the financial sectors.

This situation can be explained by many factors. One of them is the structural heterogeneity exhibited by Latin American economies for historical reasons. Another is the traditional gulf between industry and agriculture and the spread of a kind of self-fulfilling prophecy in the sense that agriculture has always been thought to be immune to market stimuli and condemned to remain locked into traditional systems of production. This idea has held sway even though international experience indicates that modern agriculture or agribusiness has a heretofore unsuspected potential for diversification and growth and that satisfactory interaction between agriculture and industry tends to promote a vigorous insertion into international trade through new and highly competitive agricultural products or agriculturally-based manufactures. Another factor is the inward orientation of Latin American development processes in this century: during the import substitution stage, many products that international experience would have considered tradable, proved to be otherwise, owing to their poor quality and the high cost of producing them, which ultimately halted the export process.

Another of these dichotomies is the gap between the productive activities arduously developed by the countries of the region and the development of a satisfactory transportation and communications infrastructure, modern marketing systems, and a solid foundation in telecommunications and information processing. Another false dilemma has long been the exaggerated separation of production for export and production oriented toward satisfying the countries' domestic needs. This dilemma refers fundamentally to agriculture and food production, which if stimulated, while at the same time ensuring a nation's food supply, can generate new lines of export products through specialized production (fruit, flowers or fish, for example) or through agroindustry. Moving beyond these dichotomies and enhancing the intersectoral integration of Latin America's economies is another key prerequisite for improving the countries' international competitiveness.

Just as it is impossible to expect a strongly competitive country to exhibit similar efficiency levels across the board in all sectors of its economy, competitive industries in a given economy do not necessarily tend to concentrate in a limited range of interrelated sectors. On the contrary, there is usually a considerable degree of dispersion. This is because excellence and competitiveness are not always associated with the pursuit of sectorally-focused policies. Instead, they are often the fruit of individual success stories, within the general framework of adequate policies and a climate that favors innovation and enhanced productivity. A look at the world's major economies reveals that the United States is especially competitive in the areas of engineering and construction equipment, refrigeration and air conditioning equipment, chemical products, monitoring and control instruments, computer hardware and software, commercial aviation, waste disposal equipment, advertising, and the film industry; the United Kingdom has an advantage in the areas of chemical and pharmaceutical products, electrical generators, apparel, insurance, pastries, and the auction industry; Germany, in automobiles, chemical products, optical instruments, bottling and packaging equipment, and x-ray and printing equipment; Italy, in household appliances, industrial automation, ceramics, theater equipment, wool manufactures, shoes, and ski boots; and Japan, in audio and video equipment, carbon fibers, synthetic fibers, fax machines, microwave and satellite communications equipment, musical instruments, robotics, ship building, and automobile and truck manufactures. Within the same product line, the competitive advantage tends to be distributed differently in different countries. For example, German automobile exports concentrate on high-quality cars, while Korea's specialize in inexpensive compact models; Japan holds a strong footing in general machinery and equipment, while Italy has an edge in highly specialized machinery.

The same holds true in Latin America, where countries like Brazil have developed a competitive advantage in specific sectors as diverse as poultry complexes, information processing for banking activities, and orange juice production; Chile, in agroindustrial

Increasing competitiveness as a diffuse process

production, seafood products, and computer software; and Uruguay, in leather goods, wool, and ceramics, while gaining an edge with the recent growth of an agroindustrial complex for the export of dairy products. The apparently surprising and diverse nature of competitive advantage in particular countries and sectors is nearly always the result of a combination of a healthy economic climate and successful grassroots initiatives. A country can be said to have embarked on the road toward international competitiveness when a growing number of its economic players see the possibilities in this combination or interaction, begin to have confidence in it, and apply it to their own productive activities. This type of change generally occurs at a more provincial than universal level.

In an ever-more dynamic, diversified, and complex economy, productivity depends mainly on the level of know-how or technology incorporated into the productive processes and related services. Technological modernization is essential both for the efficiency of productive operations and for the services required to carry out operations and incorporate them into the rest of the economy—from prospecting for natural resources and processing raw materials to advertising, marketing, and financial services, education, transportation, and communications.

Knowledge and technological innovation; keys to competitiveness

Moreover, the prevailing technologies at each stage of world economic development are grounded in a number of common features derived from a given technological paradigm.[41] Schumpeter referred to radical innovations capable of transforming the entire productive apparatus, based on a new combination of natural resources, technologies, entrepreneurial skill, and forms of social organization. It has also been observed that each of these revolutions culminates in the emergence of a new technological paradigm, grounded in some common element or elements that are not only abundant and cheap but have multiple uses and can be found at the heart of numerous productive processes. During the first industrial revolution, these elements were coal and steel. Later, they were petroleum and its derivatives. Today, they are information and microelectronics. Finally, to take advantage of the universality of these latter elements and the ease with which they can be utilized in the various branches of the economy, they must be sectorally integrated to enable innovation, their incorporation into the heart of the

[41] H. Khun, *The Structure of Scientific Revolutions*, 1962, and C. Ominami, ed., *La tercera revolución industrial: Impactos internacionales del actual viraje tecnológico*, Buenos Aires, Rial, 1987.

various branches of technology, and their diffusion throughout the different sectors of society and the economy, in as orderly a manner as possible. Adopting this process will generate productivity levels that are mutually compatible, instead of heterogeneous, and shared by all sectors and agents within the economy.

Incorporating technological innovation is vital to the countries' competitiveness, for it constitutes an essentially relative concept, presuming to compare a country's forms of production with the best systems in the world market for particular types of goods or services. Thus, it is inevitable that superior or inferior technologies, processes, or products exist side by side in both the enterprises of different countries and those of a single country. Technology, moreover, cannot be regarded as an inventory of knowledge that a country can develop or acquire either gratis or for a price and incorporate into its system of production. Competition constantly induces changes in productive techniques and processes, making technological innovation more an ability than an acquisition. Finally, since technology is not free economic property and, under the current system of industrial property rights, it is increasingly less so, companies that develop or incorporate a given innovation gain a lasting advantage in the market. This advantage constitutes both an incentive and a source of income, though in the long run it can disappear if the company fails to remain at the forefront of technological change.

World trade in manufactures has been expanding at a faster pace than total trade, especially for goods that contain a higher degree of technological innovation. However, products that reflect greater technological efficiency and, hence, greater vigor in international trade, undergo modifications as technology changes. Each country's competitiveness therefore depends largely on its ability to keep up with international technological developments. Hence, we see the recent emphasis on the importance of the only dynamic production factor that is inexhaustible: incorporating new knowledge into the productive processes, including upgrading the work force and improving the organization of enterprises.

Technology and international trade

This trend highlights the importance of the response capability of Latin American countries to the challenges of the external environment and to the demands of their own development processes. "The globalization of industries and the internationalization of companies leaves us with a paradox. It is tempting to conclude that the nation has lost its role in the international success of its firms. Companies, at first glance, seem to have transcended countries. Yet [...] this study contradicts this conclusion. As earlier examples have suggested, the leaders in particular industries and segments of indus-

Creating competitive advantages

91

tries tend to be concentrated in a few nations and sustain competitive advantage for many decades. When firms from different nations form alliances, those firms based in nations which support true competitive advantage eventually emerge as the unambiguous leaders.

Competitive advantage is created and sustained through a highly localized process. Differences in national economic structures, values, cultures, institutions, and histories contribute profoundly to competitive success. The role of the home nation seems to be as strong or stronger than ever. While globalization of competition might appear to make the nation less important, instead it seems to make it more so. With fewer impediments to trade to shelter uncompetitive domestic firms and industries, the home nation takes on growing significance because it is the source of the skills and technology that underpin competitive advantage."[42]

The systemic nature of the process

Hence, the insistence with which current Latin American thought argues that enhancing competitiveness is a systemic process. From the standpoint of incorporating technological advances into productive processes, an economy's performance does not depend solely on the reaction of business to changes in the price system. Rather, it relies on a set of highly complex factors and externalities. In this process, the know-how acquired by certain sectors, enterprises, or workers tends to pass from one sector to another, creating an environment or context favorable to the transmission of these innovations.

The intersectoral integration of the economies acquires its true value here, as does the homogeneity with which technological innovation is disseminated throughout all branches of the economy, thereby increasing the flexibility of each branch to respond and adapt to economic signals and complement them with other productive activities or the services necessary for its development. Another highly important element is the interaction that should exist between technological factors, and the various institutions and economic and social sectors or players. Schumpeter had already made the distinction between technological discovery or innovation, strictly speaking, and its economic applications and dissemination throughout society and the economy as a whole.

---

[42] M. E. Porter, op. cit., pp. 18-19.

The role of the various players

One of the key dynamic forces within the industrialized economies this century has been the close linkage between government, private enterprise, and scientific institutions—particularly in response to major emergencies, like the Great Depression of the 1930s or the two world wars, which gave rise in their day to the military industrial complex, of which so much has been said. It might be asserted that one of the causes and characteristics of underdevelopment is precisely a lack of interaction between the above-mentioned sectors.

Interaction between the various players

Over 20 years ago, the late Argentine physicist Jorge Sábato denounced this situation, calling for the establishment of a solid "triangle" between the State, the scientific establishment, and the productive sectors. Today we might add to that the financial sector, to establish a kind of square—or better yet, a pyramid with four interrelated vertices. This interrelationship, in turn, underscores the importance of institutional factors or the agents of development in a strategy to raise the countries' level of international competitiveness, improve their productivity, and incorporate technological change. Such change occurs essentially at the microeconomic level and is generated and disseminated through a variety of economic and social players, both public and private.

To stimulate technological modernization, these players must interact well and become qualified through better training. As the struggle surrounding the distribution of income derived from natural resources yields ground to efforts to raise the level of competitiveness, productivity, and technological modernization, the dynamics of confrontation and conflict should be complemented or substituted with the logic of collective action, interaction, negotiation, and agreement.[43] Notwithstanding the importance of the endogenous characteristics and efforts of the various countries, in an increasingly transnational economy, adequate complementation between domestic and international players is ever more necessary.

The speed with which the processes, products, and markets that dominate the contemporary world economy change renders any arms-length relationship with the international markets unsatisfactory and obsolete. A synchronization or familiarity with them that calls for a closer institutional and personal presence than in the past is necessary. On the other hand, since access to technological inno-

Familiarity with the markets

---

[43] M. Olson, *The Logic of Collective Action,* Cambridge University Press, 1961.

vations is not free but protected by the property rights of the companies that develop them, the role of foreign investment takes on new directions that must be considered with care, especially when that role is not confined to the acquisition of previously existing assets but involves new investments that provide access to technology, products, and markets. Moreover, since the vigor of the international markets and the technological responses to their signals derive from the external environment, a strong institutional capacity for foresight at various levels of society and the State is necessary.

Since the competitive position of a country, a branch of industry, or a firm depends on its productivity, and this in turn, depends essentially on its ability to incorporate technological innovation in the broadest sense (which means such areas as enterprise organization, advertising, or marketing), a country's science and technology policy assumes a major role. Latin American economic thought has been very clear on this matter. The region has always been able to count on a valuable cast of characters devoted to the study and promotion of scientific and technological change—personalities like Jorge Sábato, Máximo Halty-Carrier, or Manuel Noriega Morales, to name but a few of those who are no longer with us. In the face of the emergencies that our governments have traditionally had to confront in the short term, it frequently fell to these thinkers to be unarmed prophets.

The relative magnitude of each country's efforts in the field of science and technology depends on highly complex factors, which include, of course, its tradition and history, the extent and direction of its human resource development, and sociological factors, such as the nature of its civic culture, the extent of citizen participation, and the degree of social mobility. When observing the gulf between the various countries with regard to the resources allocated toward research and development as a share of GDP, the number of professionals highly specialized in theoretical or applied scientific disciplines, the number of academic publications that originate in the countries, the number of scientific discoveries patented by their citizens, or the research and development efforts of industrial enterprises—indicators that are very low in Latin American countries— there is a tendency to forget that all of this occurs within the framework of the conditions mentioned above.

The fact that these conditions have not developed properly in the region or have had insufficient time to develop helps explain the scant impact of intellectual concern about science and technology on the economic development of our countries. In Latin America, moreover, these conditions have not developed adequately due to the historical characteristics of the region's civic culture. In contrast to European countries that developed early trade, financial, and political systems (particularly the Anglo Saxon countries, where from the very beginning of modern times, a diversified, independent, and very dynamic civil society tended to evolve alongside the State), New World societies, largely because of their peculiar conditions, developed a more authoritarian or centralized tendency and a weaker civil society.[44] The unfettered interaction that occurs within civil society has always been a prerequisite for scientific and technological development.

These seemingly remote structural factors determined that, clarity of vision notwithstanding, Latin America's science and technology policies initially contained some rather misleading biases. Beginning in the 1960s, the first policies formulated in this area tended to concentrate exclusively on creating a scientific and technological infrastructure with strong ties to the State and/or the universities, which at that time were largely government-dependent. Recognition of the need to build a scientific and technological infrastructure was laudable, and setting it up virtually under State purview responded to the conditions of the times when the State had to assume a leadership role in promoting and planning development. International cooperation agencies like UNESCO, the IDB, and the OAS largely shared this vision, but the productive sectors of the region themselves, operating generally within protected markets, did not show great interest in participating in technological innovation, except for acquiring "turnkey" technology generated abroad.

The strategies that began to emerge at this point placed great emphasis on building or enhancing the necessary scientific and technological base for each country, which is logical given the lack of development that existed at that time. This incipient sci-tech complex consisted largely of government agencies charged with the formulation and application of science policy; public institutions devoted to research in industry, metallurgy, agriculture, nutrition, and other disciplines; institutions that began to be created at this time; and the science departments of universities that, as noted, were largely State entities. However, promoting integration between these institutions and those of the productive sector was generally ignored or given little consideration. Emphasis was instead placed on bolstering the supply of science and technology. However, as a rule, they ignored what occurred on the demand side and, above all, what was

---

[44] See C. Veliz, *The Centralist Tradition in Latin America*, Princeton, Princeton University Press, 1980.

necessary to stimulate interaction between supply and demand—interaction whose importance I must stress, because the two fronts are complementary. Furthermore, there was no clear awareness that science and technology policy should be closely coordinated with industrial, agricultural, foreign trade, and educational policies. Neither was it clear that a country's prospects for scientific and technological development are not the same when its economy is in equilibrium, its macroeconomic variables under control, the rules of the game stable, markets competitive, there is access to the financial markets, and both production and value added exhibit high growth rates.

The systematic nature of innovation in the economy

Experience indicates that, while there was a clear understanding in Latin America of this problem and deliberate policies were established to deal with it, the science and technology strategies borne of such policies suffered from the double defect of being excessively autocratic and excessively autonomous; that is, they were designed to function independently of the other economic and social variables operating in the country at a given time. To be effective, apart from being substantially correct from a technological viewpoint, these strategies must be formulated within the framework of an economy that is dynamic, competitive, and disposed to technological change. They must be closely linked to the development of the productive sectors and be integral and systemic in nature—that is, they must operate coherently throughout or within a broad spectrum of the economy. Such strategies must therefore be applied within an economy that is intersectorally integrated, and, above all, they must be based on interaction between the governmental, scientific, productive, and financial players. Since the bulk of technological innovation is produced in the large industrial sectors, and its spread to the rest of the economies and incorporation into productive enterprises is an essentially international phenomenon, this interaction must include both national entities and external players involved in the process of technological development and transfer. Creating the environment, information, and channels necessary to set up this international linkage is a difficult but essential task, if technology is to be modernized.

Linking mechanisms between the different players

Developing linking mechanisms among the various players who participate in the modernization, diffusion, and application of technology is a complex long-term process that has been an ongoing feature of the developed nations throughout their social and historical evolution, but in our own countries we must start from square one. This is the main difference between the efforts that must be undertaken today to stimulate the technological modernization of Latin

America's economies and the strategies for scientific and technological development put forward in recent decades. It is a question of strengthening technological, trade, and financial ties among specialized government agencies, scientific institutions, the agents of production—particularly small and medium-sized enterprises—and financial entities at the different levels of the economy, as well as among these players and their foreign counterparts. Establishing the appropriate mechanisms will facilitate a continuous dialogue among the different players similar to what has led to the principal technological and even cultural transformations throughout history—all of which have occurred in an atmosphere of intellectual ferment, political freedom, institutional interaction, and social participation. Such interaction is the main prerequisite for improving the investment climate in the productive sectors and accelerating the speed with which the private sector responds to the demands of growth generated by the international economic context and thus, developed within a climate of external openness. Emphasis on this process, of course, does not negate the importance of research and development efforts.

In recent decades, Latin American countries have witnessed an interesting institutional development, linked one way or another to scientific and technological progress. This development includes state agencies, such as the national councils of science and technology or institutes of applied research in specific sectors; regional and sectoral associations that represent business interests in this field; and academic organizations that in recent years have made considerable efforts to respond to the demands of the productive sector, developed applied research, and organized offices to promote or facilitate the contracting of their services by public or private enterprises. However, there is much to do to link these various players, extend this linkage to small and medium-sized economic units, and above all, facilitate access to the financial sector. Indeed, the magnitude of the resources required to promote technological change imposes constraints on Latin American enterprises. These constraints increase as the size of the enterprise decreases and become real impediments for the majority of small companies that in many other regions of the world are increasingly at the forefront of technological innovation. Hence, we see the need to convert Sábato's triangle into a square that includes the financial sectors.

Latin American countries also form part of a rich regional and international institutional structure that includes the international financial organizations, the specialized agencies of the United Nations, and diverse regional organizations that, as a rule, have their own priorities, programs, and mechanisms in this field. Thus, they are in a position to support new efforts at linkage between national and international entities.

What is needed is an ever-expanding number of innovative and productive initiatives that can find an appropriate organizational framework of information, contacts, negotiation, and dialogue. The framework should make it possible to explore technological solutions, share or adapt existing ones, bring together entrepreneurs in a position to help with these solutions both inside and outside the country, and search out the necessary financial resources to allow these initiatives to bear fruit. Recently, governments and international cooperation agencies have established scientific and technological development projects that share or are beginning to adopt this perspective. Among these are a group of sectoral projects financed by the Inter-American Development Bank that constitute a source of knowledge and experience.

Some specific experiences

Studies at the national and international level aimed at identifying successful models or experiences that will help surmount current barriers between production and technological research have also been carried out. Despite the extraordinary progress made in this area, the countries of the European Economic Community established the Eureka Program in 1985. The object of this program is to raise the productivity and competitiveness of their national economies in the world market by bolstering cooperation among enterprises in the various countries and between such enterprises and research institutes in the field of advanced technology. This program was the result of very specific challenges. Many of Europe's traditional industries were in decline, and entire sectors of the economy were threatened as a result of the world economic transition. Moreover, the U.S. Strategic Defense Initiative made it likely that the United States would return to the forefront of world technological development. The Eureka Program was a response to this dual challenge. Latin America confronts a challenge of a different order and magnitude that, in essence, demands that it bring itself technologically up to date.

Based on this perception, the IDB recently considered establishing a program called the Latin American Scientific and Entrepreneurial Entity (ENLACE), whose structure and goals closely pattern those of the European experience. At the same time, in October 1990, the government of Venezuela announced the launching of the Bolívar Program for Regional Technological Integration, Innovation, and Industrial Competitiveness. The two initiatives are currently linked. Their main features are an attempt to construct linking mechanisms between various national projects, based on technological innovation, promote ties between the enterprises of different countries through projects and initiatives containing scientific and technological contributions in certain fields, and stimulate technological linkage between various interrelated sectors. All countries participating in this program have created Support Councils whose composition is sufficiently broad, representative, and flexible. The institutional response of the countries to these initiatives has been very positive.

The social aspects
of development

Social development in Latin America

Poverty is a historical legacy in Latin America, aggravated by the region's traditional pattern of growth. The social stratification transferred from the centers of power to this part of the world during the colonization process, together with the lasting scars of servile labor practices and racial oppression characteristic of the societies of our hemisphere during the colonial period, left their profound mark in the form of underdevelopment, social inequality, and poverty.

Poverty: a historical legacy

    To this were added the social consequences of a development based on exports of raw materials and agricultural products and the class structure that prevailed in the region a hundred years ago.

    In the mid-nineteenth century, moreover, the region's economic and political evolution introduced new factors that exacerbated poverty. The export economy did not contribute significantly to the consolidation of domestic markets, and the social structure dominated by an exporting oligarchy gave rise to new systems of social exclusion. Reaction began to appear in the 1930s and again in the aftermath of World War II, in the form of the consolidation of the State, the emergence of industrialization, and the rise of organized labor. The trend toward the emergence of middle-income sectors later reverted toward a concentration of political power and the fruits of technical progress—a reaction, it must be acknowledged, that was in part a response to these phenomena or to the excesses of populism.

    Liberalism in Europe, the socialist revolution in what was to become the Soviet Union, and the emergence and ultimate spread of the welfare state, beginning in Great Britain under the Labor governments and in the United States under the New Deal, were reflected in Latin America in the founding of liberal or reformist political parties, the rise of the middle class, and the appearance of an organized working class after World War I. The post-World War II development model that prevailed in Latin America launched a more significant phase of social progress. This was a period of intense and sustained economic expansion, grounded in the growth and diversification of Latin America's productive capacity, the creation of a promising export potential, and a highly intense institutional development process.

Since the real gross domestic product of the region quadrupled from 1950 to 1980 while the population doubled, the real per capita product more than doubled. The social fabric became far more pluralistic, nuanced, and complex, and social stratification more diversified. The triple dichotomy between urban and rural population, workers and the middle class in the cities, and urban industrial workers and the marginally employed, so keenly analyzed during the 1950s by José Medina Echavarría, tended to break down into a multiplicity of categories without entirely disappearing. Ever-larger population groups managed to adopt the behavioral and consumption patterns of the industrialized countries, setting an important example to other groups, who increasingly tried to keep up with their conspicuous consumption. Thus, progress existed side by side with new dichotomies and significant lags.

Latin America's postwar social evolution is indissolubly linked with the progress and inadequacies of its economic development process. Social policy failures in Latin America in recent decades can often be attributed to the fact that policies were designed as if to deal with sectoral problems, or else consisted of assistance programs, instead of being part of the overall development policy. The inequalities and lags mentioned above are intimately linked to excessive external vulnerability, technological backwardness, and the inadequate vitality of Latin America's industrialization process at that time. Longstanding structural factors, which the postwar development model unsuccessfully sought to address, contributed to this backwardness—factors such as uneven income distribution, disparate educational levels, unequal opportunities among the different population groups and consequently, unequal access by the various social sectors to the fruits of progress. Large groups of Latin America's population benefited little from this progress.

The paradoxes of Latin America's postwar development manifested themselves with particular force in the social sphere. Society was characterized by the coexistence of social integration and disintegration, the incorporation and exclusion of various groups, social modernization and traditionalism, and modern homogeneity and sharp heterogeneity among the different social sectors. Despite rising emigration from the countryside to the cities, the rural population remained significant and was the most adversely affected, amassing the highest poverty rates and retaining the features of a traditional society. Urban centers grew at an extraordinary rate, as did their middle classes, while at the other end of the spectrum, the population dwelling in slums under conditions of extreme poverty and unemployment, or low-productivity employment, expanded at an equal rate. Over time, modern business attitudes and technological advances in agriculture modified the structure of rural society, creating new specialized jobs in the modern agricultural sector, expanding the supply of salaried work among women and youths, and raising family incomes, while in the traditional or *campesino* sector, the poverty and backwardness remained.

In contrast, social indicators showed remarkable improvement, with a radical decline in mortality rates, especially infant mortality, and a significant rise in life expectancy. Educational opportunities also increased (particularly in primary education but also in secondary and higher education), and there was considerably broader access to public health care, potable water and sewage services, and to a lesser extent, housing. While the number of poor rose in absolute terms, the share of the population below the critical poverty line fell significantly, especially during the 1960s.

As indicated, the crisis of the 1980s confronted Latin American countries with a sharp regression from the social standpoint, causing per capital income in the region to sink to the levels attained 13 years previously. The crisis once again brought to the fore Latin America's inequitable social structure, since the bulk of the costs of adjustment fell disproportionately on the middle and low-income groups, while the top five percent of the population retained or, in some cases, even increased its standard of living. Thus, the share of the population living under conditions of extreme poverty rose anew, largely cancelling out the progress of the 1960s and 1970s. Based on conservative estimates, the percentage of poor people rose from 41 percent in 1980 to 44 percent in 1989—that is, to 183 million inhabitants.[45] However, the permanent achievements of the progress mentioned earlier—the existing investments in physical and social infrastructure and technological advances in areas such as health— allowed for continued improvement in the social indicators on the whole, especially in the areas of infant mortality, life expectancy, education for children and youths, literacy rates, and access to water and sewage services. To some extent, the behavior of these indicators cushioned the economic decline of the poorest sectors of Latin America's population. Nonetheless, owing to the contraction in

The social development process in the 1980s

---

[45] ECLAC, *Magnitud de la pobreza en América Latina en los años 80*, Santiago, 1990, Chile, pp. 60 and 66.

investments in economic and social infrastructure and the prevailing budgetary restrictions, the crisis hurt the chances for future social advancement and opened the door to a qualitative deterioration in the services available to the population.

It should be kept in mind that the standard of living of the poorest sectors of the population depends not only on the quality of their employment and their nominal income, but fundamentally on their real income, which includes a variety of transfers and basic social services. It should also be recalled that the last decade witnessed the development of a negative concept of the State as an essentially subsidiary institution, a perception that limited the State's ability to continue to address the issue of poverty and dismantled much of its institutional capacity to do so.

In sum, while poverty is an old phenomenon in Latin America, it continued to worsen in the 1980s. The stagnation or decline of the urban sector's productive activities considerably reduced the sector's capacity to absorb labor, accentuating open unemployment or worker displacement toward less productive occupations and lowering real wages. The contraction in public expenditures resulting from the application of adjustment policies also contributed to this outcome and, above all, had an adverse effect on the quantity and quality of social services. Improved performance in the agricultural sector, in contrast, helped attenuate unemployment and probably slowed migration from rural areas to urban centers.

Poverty in the 1980s strongly increased in urban areas and was characterized by a growing heterogeneity, basically attributable to the downward social mobility unleashed by the crisis. This process was responsible for the emergence of the "nouveaux poor"—people who were poor because of their low income, not because they lacked the basic necessities of education, health care, and housing—and the growth of "chronic poverty"—people who were poor because of insufficient income and a lack of the basic necessities.[46]

Five factors related to poverty

Five factors significantly influence the evolution of poverty: demographic change, income distribution, the employment situation, the availability of social services, and the prevailing conditions in education and human resource development. Because of its importance and its intimate links with the economic growth process, this latter point will be examined separately.

Latin America is a region of rapid demographic growth. With 446 million inhabitants, the region accounts for over 8 percent

---

[46] R. Kaztman, "La heterogeneidad de la pobreza: El caso de Montevideo," *Revista de la CEPAL*, No. 37, Santiago, Chile, 1989.

of the world's population, and estimates indicate that the population will reach 526 million by the year 2000. The region's demographic behavior has exhibited major and contradictory changes. Since 1960, the average fertility rate has fallen from 6 to 3 children per woman, while at the same time, a declining mortality rate and increased life expectancy have contributed to population growth and an increment at the highest levels of the demographic pyramid. In fact, the region continues to grow faster than the world average: during the 1990s this growth is projected at 1.9 percent annually, in contrast to 1.6 percent for the rest of the world. Demographic transition has varied significantly from country to country in Latin America, from region to region, and within the social sectors of each country. In all, it can generally be said that the countries of the region will face a dual challenge: the growth in their elderly population and the equally marked growth among infants and youth. These challenges will be directed toward the services pertaining to social security, maternal and infant care, and education, as well as the training and incorporation of the younger population into the work force, within the framework of a thorough productive transformation.

Income distribution in Latin America deteriorated during the 1980s, within the context of a pronounced overall decrease in per capita income and other structural changes associated with the inequalities between different income groups and geographical areas within each country, and monetary and non-monetary benefits received by the poorest sectors of the population. A study by ECLAC in Argentina, Brazil, Colombia, Costa Rica, Uruguay, and Venezuela examining household income distribution by quartiles of family income per capita—with considerable variations from country to country—shows a downward trend in income levels in the majority of these countries (or a return to pre-1980 income levels, as in the case of Brazil). It also shows a rising disparity in distribution of the income between the lowest and highest quartiles of the population, and between rural and urban zones.[47]

The crisis of the 1980s, moreover, seriously affected employment levels. This was due to the sharp decrease in the capacity to absorb labor in the urban productive sectors that provide the most stable, productive and better remunerated jobs with the highest social security benefits; the sharp decline in real wages; and the way that governments reacted in terms of policies and legislation in this area,

---

[47] ECLAC, "Nota sobre el desarrollo social en América Latina." Report of the Executive Director of ECLAC at the First Conference of Latin American Chiefs of State, in Guadalajara, Mexico, July 16-19, 1991.

within the framework of economic adjustment and productive re-structuring policies that deregulated the labor markets and/or adversely affected real wages.

In the past, the sustained growth of Latin America's economies was accompanied by a rising absorption of the more productive and qualified human resources by the modern sectors of the economy, while the economically-active population in agriculture fell. This occupational mobility stimulated growth in productive and well-paid jobs in the formal sector, especially among salaried employees in large and medium-sized enterprises, and in the public sector. The recent crisis produced an inverse trend, transferring labor from the more productive and remunerative jobs to other occupations that were inferior, with a stagnation in opportunities for social mobility and the descent of households to lower rungs on the social ladder. Even though agriculture, as noted, made a positive contribution to job creation, employment in the service and informal sectors rose sharply, with an average per capita productivity of 20 percent below that of 1980, while unemployment in the urban industrial sector doubled. It seems likely that the majority of the newly poor constitute self-employed professionals and workers from the manufacturing industry and the public sector.

Apart from the evolution of employment in the agricultural sector, one of the positive trends that should be mentioned is the rising number of non-professionals who are self-employed or working in small enterprises—a figure that increased 25 percent more than that of overall employment. Generally speaking, it can be said that the crisis seriously hindered the progress of the modern sector of the economies, displacing major sectors of the work force with less productive, less stable, and lower paying jobs that provide little coverage from the standpoint of social security, and concentrating new opportunities in the informal sector, self-employment, and medium-sized and small enterprises.

Fiscal constraints and a decrease in public employment, among other things, seriously affected the coverage and, above all, the quality of the services provided by public agencies, particularly in the social sector. It should be noted that the governments have made great efforts to soften the impact of fiscal constraints on the provision of basic social services. Indeed, social expenditures remained the same or even increased as a share of overall fiscal expenditures, but since the latter contracted, social expenditures declined in absolute terms. Among the main characteristics of this phenomenon are that investments in social services fell more than current expenditures in this field; that cutbacks in housing, health, and education were more severe than in social security; and that in any case, this latter sector finds itself in serious financial difficulties.[48]

In the short term, these measures reinforced the cycle of deterioration. In the longer term, the decline in investment in human capital formation may have severe consequences for the region's growth potential.

There are both economic and ethical reasons for attacking these problems. One hundred years ago, the Pope sent a message to humanity on this subject that remains valid today. Both types of considerations must be taken into account, for, as the great economic historians and sociologists of modern times have shown, from Weber and Sombart to Drucker and Porter, the incentive to develop is in essence always a question of attitude.

Old and new aspects of the problem

Nevertheless, there are more reasons than ever to conclude that improving social conditions is probably the main prerequisite for growth, given the direction that this process has taken. In fact, inasmuch as the engine of growth has become creativity, technological change, the ability to organize social and economic activities in a modern fashion, economic openness, and the countries' international competitiveness, the social terrain in which these aptitudes can put down roots becomes absolutely essential for their success.

The social question is indeed an old problem, aggravated in Latin America by the economic crisis and structural adjustments. However, it is also true that in addition to the unmet challenge of critical poverty, there is now the need to create a social structure in the broadest sense, to accompany and support the economic reforms to which our countries are committed, facilitating the incorporation of all sectors into the productive process. Meeting both challenges is essential to stabilize and ensure the success of the economic strategies that our countries are pursuing in response to pressures from legitimate social concerns.

Therefore, the tasks that confront our nations in this respect are twofold. First, and with dramatic urgency, the enormous social debt generated by the inexorable demands of the 1980s must be settled, through the appropriate compensatory measures. Second, progress must be made toward new levels of integration that will permit all threads of the social fabric to be woven into the rich tapestry of today's productive process. These are two undertakings whose effects are concentrated primarily in the short term, for the first point, and in the medium and long term, for the second.

---

[48] IDB, *Economic and Social Progress in Latin America,* 1991 edition.

Strategies to combat poverty

*Growth and
poverty*

During the 1950s and 1960s, economic growth was considered the principal way to reduce poverty, providing the poor with access to the opportunities presented by progress and improving their quality of life. Confidence in the "trickle down effect" was, in some cases, an extreme manifestation of this approach. In the 1970s, doubts were raised about the ability of growth to raise the level of welfare among the poor. The emphasis was on projects specifically oriented toward generating employment in the poorer sectors and on the provision of basic services in housing, health care, and education—services whose distribution as public goods effectively raised the income of the poor. The Carter Administration in the United States underscored the need for the benefits of international cooperation to directly reach the poorest sectors of the population. In the 1980s, however, the debt crisis and the need to implement drastic adjustment measures— phenomena that in some cases coincided with political regimes that were hardly participatory—detracted from these concerns. The distancing of the international financial agencies from these problems and the temptation to concentrate on re-establishing macroeconomic stability, coupled with pressure on Latin American governments to service their foreign debt and put their economies in order, helped further this serious neglect. A return to balancing the requirements of equity and growth is needed if this situation is to be remedied with social concerns placed at the core of new development strategies.

*Society's
commitment*

Experience indicates that economic growth will not resolve the problem of poverty unless accompanied by deep social concern, and that redistributive policies, be they the distribution of wealth, increased social services, or the granting of subsidies, will not be effective either, if there is no increase in the product to distribute. Here, as always, it is useful to examine past experiences, since some strategies have been more successful than others. Almost all successful strategies have been based on the simultaneous application of two elements: the intelligent and intensive use of the only productive factor that the poor possess—their labor—complemented by better-targeted social services. In some countries, economic growth has led to a certain increment in income among the poor, although some basic indicators, such as life expectancy, infant mortality, and education, remain precarious. Other countries have stressed services, but growth has been too slow, compromising the income of the poor and, in the final analysis, limiting the possibilities of continuing to provide them with social benefits.

Achieving a satisfactory combination of greater participation by the poorest sectors in the productive process and the provision of more basic social services to them assumes a commitment on the part of society to overcome poverty, for this combination involves major compromises. These compromises do not require choosing between greater growth or greater poverty alleviation, as it was formerly believed. The two objectives are not mutually exclusive. Increased productive use of the work force and greater investment in human capital are not only compatible with an efficient development strategy, they are a prerequisite for it. However, since such measures imply channeling a larger share of the national income and public expenditures toward the poorer segments of society, these accommodations lie between the interests of those sectors and those that are better off. This strategy will therefore be more viable in countries where the poor have a greater say in the decision-making process, and where the more affluent have learned to make their interests compatible with those of the poor.

Diverse strategies

Thus, the chief prerequisite for overcoming poverty is for society as a whole to develop democratic consensus-building processes conducive to greater social cohesion and to make commitments that favor growing equity in the distribution of the benefits of economic growth. It is no accident that poverty, as a rule, has risen under authoritarian regimes that allow for little participation, and that, historically, overcoming poverty has been facilitated under stable, democratic systems with the broadest possible social base and oriented toward the search for consensus and compromise.

The two elements of the above-mentioned strategy are inseparable, for greater productive participation by the work force in the economy cannot be fostered without an increase in basic social services and additional investment in human capital. There is no single recipe for achieving this last objective. Some strategies have stressed the redistribution of wealth (particularly land), with varying degrees of success, while in others, preference has been given to strengthening public investment in human resource development. Both strategies have a positive impact on the poor, and both can affect the rate of economic growth, at least in the short term. The redistribution of wealth can place constraints on economic efficiency and productivity, at least temporarily, and investment in human resources presupposes an increase in taxes and public expenditures that may hinder growth for a time. Moreover, both strategies tend to work against the interests of the groups that are most powerful—though the redistribution of assets may have a more alarming effect.

Income distribution and wealth

109

These goals can be achieved in various ways. One consists of redistributing the existing wealth; another, of increasing the share of new investments aimed at providing basic social services and upgrading human resources. Naturally, these investments will produce the desired economic and social results only insofar as the economy opens up new opportunities that incorporate the work force productively. Economic growth and social equity are thus inseparable. In this respect, it is important to note that there is a way to redistribute wealth that does not involve the transfer of assets. It consists, rather, of making investments that are conducive to an improvement in the yield and profitability of the activities in which the majority of the poor are employed—for example, agricultural or informal sector activities.

Better use of the work force

The rise in income among the poorer sectors can be explained in part by overall economic growth and in part by changes in income distribution. Taking advantage of both presupposes an adequate combination of numerous factors. Policies aimed at incorporating the poorer sectors into the economic growth process essentially include providing them with greater access to ownership of the land and/or an increase in the profitability of agricultural activities; access to greater credit, which often involves the creation of financial institutions for these sectors; and greater access to the countries' existing physical and social infrastructure, as well as to the technology appropriate to their work activities. The majority of these measures, like those oriented toward income redistribution, presuppose public investment and, as a result, transactions among the various income groups that influence the respective political systems.

Basic social services

The effective use of the abundant labor force in our countries, however, depends not only on investments but on new forms of production and organization. This requires the establishment of major flows of technical assistance to the poorest workers, the informal sectors, and microenterprises—assistance that could be offered through adequate coordination of efforts between the public and private sectors. Experience indicates, furthermore, that conditions in the urban and rural sectors are very different and, hence, so are the respective measures that should be adopted. Similarly, today there is a great deal of experience with regard to the need to institute special support policies for the more depressed regions in a given country or group of countries, as was the case in northeast Brazil or the "Mezzogiorno" in Europe.

Another group of policies centers around redistributing benefits to favor the poorest segments of society, which requires action in the fields of health, nutrition, and education, plus greater access to public services—especially social services (including the administration of justice, the modernization of which has proven to have a significant impact in solving certain social problems).

Several specific issues must be addressed when applying these policies. Probably most important is the training, organization, and incorporation of youth into productive occupations. Another is the impact of technological change on women's work, where the transformation and diversification of the productive structure is opening up new opportunities that will require educational, organizational, and legal measures if they are to be fully exploited. Measures that involve the labor markets, educational systems, and the legal system are needed to provide new opportunities for youth. A development strategy that promotes the incorporation of the work force into productive occupations within a framework of major structural reforms should have some impact on rural migration to urban areas. In the past, this population movement fueled excessive and costly growth in urban centers without substantially alleviating poverty, serving instead simply to change its venue.

From this standpoint, industrial development policies in the urban sector are very important—especially those referring to the markets for goods, capital, and labor. Very often, inadequate government intervention in these markets has accentuated the bias against the use of labor in the structured, or formal, sectors. This occurs when governments make imports of capital goods cheaper, discouraging the use of existing labor; when tariff or exchange rate policies hinder exports, to the detriment of a more open trade policy that favors job creation; or when excessive regulation of the labor market raises barriers to the creation of new jobs. While there are differences from country to country, the informal sector in the majority of Latin American economies has grown significantly; no longer perceived as a problem—a pocket of hidden poverty or unproductive work—it is now regarded as a major source of labor and income, often accompanied by a considerable endogenous organizational capacity. Thus, the sector must constitute a key target of not only social policy but also of the countries' development strategy and an important area for concentrating efforts toward human resource development.

As we have noted, all of these measures imply investments or expenditures in one way or another, with substantial public sector participation. The degree to which these expenditures threaten the macroeconomic stability of a country will not only compromise the success of its development strategy, but will also hurt the poorest sectors of society through an inflation tax. It is therefore of the utmost importance to establish certain guidelines to prevent this from hap-

Attack on poverty: investment needs

111

pening. One such guideline is related to the greater investment possibilities that would derive from a decrease in the transfer of our countries' resources through the external debt service. Others have to do with the our countries' tax systems, where it will be necessary to broaden the tax base, reduce tax evasion, and target the use of taxes increasingly toward measures like those cited above, preventing the new resources from favoring the upper and middle classes. Another concerns the efficiency of the State apparatus, where spending will have to be redirected away from certain high-cost activities that serve the needs of society's middle and upper classes and toward the needs of the poor. Furthermore, government must put an end to subsidies to productive sectors devoted to activities that are nonessential, poorly managed, or inefficient. Reductions in military spending, particularly in light of new global strategic relations, will be another inevitable step under the new Latin American development strategies.

Upgrading human resources

The importance of human resources in promoting growth and combatting poverty

Among the policies aimed at improving the situation of the poorer sectors and making economic growth compatible with social concerns, none perhaps is more important than upgrading human resources and incorporating them into the productive system. The past decade has been characterized by a growing insertion of the Latin American economies into the world markets, together with new demands with regard to the quality of their macroeconomic policies, the modernization of their productive structures, and the competitiveness of their exports—all of which require new knowledge, technological innovation, new organizational forms, and better qualified human resources. At the same time, the relatively higher levels of welfare and complexity in Latin American countries following the postwar period of growth has accentuated the internal stratification within their societies, favored the emergence of various interest groups, and furthered distributional struggles, as it has in the industrialized societies—albeit to a lesser degree.[49] Consequently, the identity and the interests of the different groups depends increasingly

---

[49] See M. Olson, *The Logic of Collective Action*, Cambridge University Press, 1961, and *The Rise and Decline of Nations: Stagflation, and Social Rigidities*, New Haven, Yale University Press, 1982.

on their technical know-how, skill at developing proposals, and ability to negotiate agreements with the government or other social groups. Finally, the trend toward increasing the professionalism and technical knowledge of authorities in the executive branch, the parliaments, and other representative bodies, necesitated by the growing complexity of modern life, makes it possible that the groups represented will have less to say in the handling of their own problems unless they assume greater responsibility and become more technically competent. This combination of economic, social, and political factors underscores the importance of human resources in Latin America's current economic and political development.

The economic reforms underway in Latin America have three features in common that call for the readaptation of the work force: the search for fiscal equilibrium, the gradual transfer of the dynamic growth forces from the State to the private sector, and the opening of the economies to international trade.[50] One of the main lessons that Latin American countries have learned during the 1980s has been the need to maintain fiscal equilibrium as a precondition to lowering inflation and stabilizing the economy. This was the experience of Mexico, which decreased its inflation rate from nearly 160 percent to less than 20 percent, moving from a fiscal deficit equivalent to 7 percent of its GDP to a surplus of the same magnitude. Bolivia, Colombia, Chile, and Venezuela had similar experiences. Fiscal equilibrium is achieved by simultaneously controlling expenditures and income. Since salaries constitute the bulk of public spending, reducing the State payroll—whether by lowering wages or decreasing the number of public employees—has become an inevitable component of this policy. From 1983 to 1991, real wages in the public sector in Argentina were reduced by one-half. The alternative is to reduce the number of state employees, which means transfering some of them to the private sector.

The need to readapt the work force

The economic reforms underway in Latin America tend to assign a much more vital role to the private sector than in the past. The privatization of certain services or productive activities is one of the main components of these reforms. One of the reasons for the inefficiency of public enterprises has sometimes been their tendency to retain an excessive number of personnel. Thus, privatization will often require a reduction in personnel, and insofar as possible, the opening up of work opportunities in other areas.

---

[50] W. R. Cline, "Facilitating Labor Adjustment in Latin America," document prepared for the IDB in October 1991 (unpublished).

Finally, the impact of trade liberalization should be taken into account. The import substitution strategy promoted and protected certain sectors for long periods of time. Trade liberalization implies greater competitiveness, with a consequent decline in less competitive sectors and a rise in those able to develop new comparative advantages. This, in turn, requires a transfer of resources toward sectors able to substitute imports more efficiently or toward new exporting sectors. At the same time, since reducing external deficits presupposes that the production of nontradable goods is to be gradually displaced by that of tradable goods, additional pressure toward job displacement will be generated. In all such cases, there may be a discontinuity or gap between the elimination of jobs in traditional sectors and the creation of new opportunities in emerging sectors.

This issue is therefore cause for great international concern. In the majority of the advanced countries, including those that are very different from the standpoint of size or economic structure, there is evidence of a growing recognition of the importance of educational systems in the economic growth process and, in general, in the behavior of economic and social systems. The worldwide process of economic, political, and cultural transformation has created the need to mold values, attitudes, and social behavior to the realities of the future, exposing the lags, deficiencies, and limitations of the countries' educational systems and underscoring the need to adapt them to these demands.[51]

This leads to some conclusions that should be borne in mind when discussing Latin America. First, since the major demands on the educational system derive from technological and productive transformation and the winds of change, modern societies must possess a strong and duly institutionalized capacity for foresight and provision, as indicated by the experience of Japan, a nation that rebuilt itself with a view toward the future, principally through MITI. Second, all of the countries that have considered or instituted educational reforms have done so within their respective traditions, learning more from their own experience than from copying foreign models. Third, all of these countries have given priority to the

---

[51] See A. Bloom, *The Closing of the American Mind,* New York, Simon and Schuster, 1987; National Commission on Excellence in Education, *A Nation at Risk,* Washington, D.C., 1983; and U.S. Department of Education, *America 2000: An Educational Strategy,* Washington, D.C., 1991; see also I. Suzuki, "La reforma educativa en el Japón con miras al Siglo XXI," in *Perspectivas,* Volume XX, No. 1, 1990, and J. Lesournne, *Education et Societé: Les Défis de L'An 2000,* Paris, 1988.

institutional transformations needed to improve the quality of education—that is, the creation of modern, efficient, and flexible organizational and management mechanisms in education, in contrast to the highly bureaucratic educational systems of the past. Fourth, any efforts to modernize these systems that are not accompanied by a vigorous process of democratization in education and the creation of the greatest possible number of opportunities for society as a whole will lose much of their impact on stimulating development. Fifth, adjustments must be made in close alliance with the productive sectors and with their cooperation.

Finally, for the reasons cited above, educational modernization, to be successful, requires the broadest possible political and social consensus.

It is especially important to establish close ties between the educational system and programs to develop human resources, on the one hand, and the business sector, on the other, for it is here that changes in the productive structure, technological innovations, organizational systems, and new labor needs are generated. It is at this level that integration between educational systems and productive structures should take place. The private sector in Latin America, therefore, has an important role to play. In the past, however, it has not done so, and if it is to assume its responsibilities in this field, well-defined public policies that include direction and stimulus from the State are necessary.

Rapprochement between business and the educational system

In recent years, in addition to the changes that have occurred in the international insertion of Latin America's economies and in their productive structures, the lack of synchronization between educational systems and the countries' development processes has become more pronounced. Most of all, the inequalities in educational systems have grown, as middle- and upper-level income groups have taken advantage of opportunities to pressure governments to target a substantial portion of public investment in education toward their own children. Thus, education, which has historically been the principal means of upward mobility in Latin American countries, has gradually lost this capacity, while fiscal resources have made possible free education at the highest levels for the upper-income sectors. At the same time, the unfortunate combination of the trend toward centralizing and bureaucratizing educational systems and the fiscal constraints facing our countries in the 1980s have resulted in a tangible decline in the quality of education at all levels; although coverage at the primary, secondary, and university levels has been maintained or expanded, the quality of the training received by young people has profoundly deteriorated, has recurred increasingly to rote learning, and has gradually dissociated itself from the demands of a modern society based on new types of information, organization, and productive structures.

Another negative tendency is the progressive segmentation and disjointedness found in the various educational levels and disciplines—the result of isolated responses by the respective systems to the new pressures. New educational establishments have been added horizontally and new training levels (pre-school, technical, or post-graduate) vertically, with few links among them and a serious lack of coherence, together with mechanisms designed to attend separately to the different sectors of the social hierarchy. The main result of these negative trends has been a growing gap between education and development.

Magnitude of worker displacement required by the productive changes

A recent study provides some general estimates of the magnitude of labor displacement that could result from economic reforms.[52] Public sector employment accounts for some 20 percent of the work force in Latin American countries, and wages in this sector for about 10 percent of GDP. The discrepancy between the two figures can be explained not so much by the fact that wages in the public sector are comparatively lower than those in the private sector, but that the share of wages in GDP in the region does not exceed 50 percent. This situation varies from country to country; remunerations in the public sector represent 10 percent of GDP in Argentina and 5.5 percent in Chile. Given the weight of government remunerations in public expenditures, achieving a reasonable fiscal equilibrium in the Latin American countries would require reducing these expenditures, on average, to a little more than one-half of their present size. This would imply a displacement of between 5 and 10 percent of the work force toward new sectors, depending on the country. This massive transfer is likely to be greater, if there is an attempt to recover the levels of real wages in government jobs. This implies challenges of a considerable magnitude, if we take into account the new responsibilities that the States must assume to facilitate the economic reforms, as well as the fact that in the industrialized countries of Europe, public sector remunerations account for no less than 10 percent of GDP.

The other source of labor displacement is the trend toward economic openness. If we consider that 15 percent of Latin America's work force is employed in the manufacturing sector and that because of international competition, up to 10 percent should be transferred to new productive sectors, this would imply a transfer of another 1.5

---

[52] W.R. Cline, op. cit.

percent of the Latin American work force. Using the most favorable estimates, this means that probably about 10 million workers would be displaced from one job to another. If we assume that the cost of the training programs required to readapt these workers represents one-quarter of the average wage per worker, about $1,000 per displaced worker would be required—that is, roughly $10 billion, which would translate into an increment of about 20 percent in current educational expenditures by the State, the private sector, and families.[53]

The policies needed to overcome this dichotomy presuppose a reevaluation of the importance of education and human resources in development strategies; a vigorous and flexible attempt to identify the needs imposed by the changing productive structure of the work force; the creation of an institutional structure able to respond in an equally flexible manner to these needs and open to the innovations required by them; ensuring that these institutions are endowed with an efficient, agile, and adaptable administration; upgrading educators and bolstering their professionalism; guaranteeing more universal access by all social sectors to the new training facilities; promoting collaboration between the public and private sector, as well as between central, regional, and local institutions in the development of the new educational program; and promoting a commitment by society and the State to finance this program.

Education and human resources: diverse approaches

The aforementioned study, commissioned by the IDB, presents three basic prototypes for labor adjustment programs. The modality that is most directly and easily applied to displaced workers in the public sector is compensation for the loss of the job. Political considerations aside, the economic justification for this strategy would depend on such compensation being less than the cost of remuneration for a job completely lacking in social productivity—a condition difficult to meet. Apart from the fact that this formula can turn out to be extremely costly, conventional economic theory's presumption that the laid-off worker will maximize the use of his indemnization and obtain the necessary training to seek another position is extremely dubious under the current social conditions in Latin America.

---

[53] A recent ECLAC study in this area estimates that the increase in educational expenditures as a share of GDP would represent almost three times the figure just cited; that is, 13.5 percent, which, added to the 6.5 percent that the countries currently allocate to education, would total about 20 percent of the GDP—a figure comparable to that of some industrialized nations, but below the efforts of Korea or Taiwan in this field. See ECLAC, *Educación y conocimiento: Eje de la transformación productiva con equidad,* Santiago, Chile, 1991.

Emergency or minumum employment programs are a second possibility. Used by the U.S. government in the 1930s during the Great Depression and by Chile for a time during the military regime, they are supposedly cheaper than indemnifying workers and can be targeted toward low-income sectors and channeled into the creation of social capital through public works. Experience, however, indicates that these programs tend to be economically unproductive, provide little retraining for displaced workers, and are socially degrading. This formula, in principle, bears no relation to the need to readapt the worker to the conditions generated by economic reforms. It is basically an attempt to replace certain more traditional public jobs with new, unproductive forms of government employment.

A third strategy is to train displaced workers to fill new jobs that are more in line with the productive reconstruction under way. Given the generally systemic nature of transformation within a productive system, as well as the need to readapt the work force to the new demands generated by the transformation, there are no compelling reasons to justify confining this solution to displaced workers from the public sector.

Naturally, when compared to the two other formulas, particularly the second, this approach has a disadvantage in that it fails to guarantee new jobs. However, it has the advantage of concentrating efforts on training the worker in jobs that are truly productive within the emerging economic structure. Clearly, such an approach requires not only an enormous effort and mobilization of resources, but also an integral approach to the problem, which would represent a real cultural revolution in each country. From this standpoint, the magnitude of the material and financial effort required to carry out this task may not be what is most decisive. Rather, it is the qualitative aspects related to the introduction of institutional innovations into the educational system at all levels; the increased know-how of the players involved in the educational process; the broadening of the concept of who these players are, to include not only public sector educational institutions but also the business community, the mass media, and families; and in general, a change in attitudes and greater social motivation with regard to the educational process.

Operational recommendations

A recent conference on this topic arrived at a set of conclusions on how to most effectively channel resources toward a program to upgrade human resources in Latin America.[54] Among them are the

---

[54] Conference on human resources in the adjustment processes, organized by the IDB, September 20, 1991.

following recommendations: adopt a comprehensive approach that integrates educational adaptation, social integration, and economic growth within a single strategy; orient interventions in this area toward very specific groups that, in principle, will include small- and medium-sized enterprises and the informal sector; focus special attention on rehabilitating workers displaced from their traditional jobs and consider the possibility of establishing social security networks that include facilitating the rapid placement of workers in new productive occupations among their objectives; ensure that programs have the broadest possible training base, oriented toward providing workers with the basic skills needed to incorporate themselves into a rapidly changing labor market, and that such programs maintain permanent flexibility from the standpoint of educational institutions and their programs; orient programs toward the new employment opportunities generated by the productive restructuring of the countries, taking into account the specific endowment of factors in each country; link private sector efforts to these initiatives; and explore the possibility of creating national funds to finance these programs with contributions from public, private, and international sources.

It is interesting to note that while concern about upgrading human resources within the above-mentioned parameters is relatively new in Latin America, many countries have had valuable experiences of different types in the areas mentioned, with diverse orientations. From a substantive viewpoint, these experiences include efforts to upgrade primary and intermediate education; the provision of basic adult education; specialized technical training programs and/or programs targeted towards specific groups; special programs for the sectors that have been more severely affected, and on-site training programs in enterprises or programs based on a combination of efforts between the public and private sector.

The Enterprise for the Americas Initiative proposes the establishment of a Multilateral Investment Fund aimed at promoting structural reforms in the Latin American economies. Its emphasis is on improving the conditions necessary for stimulating private investment, to which it assigns a more important role in the economic development of the region than it has had in the past. Contributions by the donor countries to this Fund amount to $1.5 billion, to be used within a five-year period, largely in the form of concessional financing. The Fund has three windows: a technical assistance program, a program to foster enterprise development, and another for human resource development. Bearing in mind that technical asssistance activities by definition require fewer resources, this latter program

The Multilateral Investment Fund

could channel roughly one-half of the funds available from the Initiative. Comparing this figure with the medium-term cost of readapting human resources in Latin America, based on the previously formulated conjectures, we can conclude that the contribution of these resources to this task would be relatively small.

This implies that the program must attempt to produce a catalytic effect, helping to create the conditions necessary for the success of other national or international efforts in the same direction. This is no understatement, for obstacles as important as the magnitude of the resources required to resolve this problem are the incipient nature of the reforms underway in this area in the countries, their lack of experience in education applied to the training and rehabilitation of the work force, or the inadequate quality of the existing projects in this area. Hence, the use of these funds must be linked to two basic conditions: the existence of feasible economic reform programs in the productive sectors and in trade, and the development of innovative projects to adapt human resources to the demands of these reforms.

With regard to the possibilities of mobilizing the necessary resources to carry out this task, within which the Enterprise for the Americas Initiative would represent but a modest fraction, it should be recalled that taking on this challenge could not be considered without a commitment at the national level of resources by government, the private sector, local or grassroots communities, families, and the mass media. We must also bear in mind that bilateral and multilateral sources of international financing are available for these ends, and that their activities ordinarily linked with the educational systems can be channeled towards the new programs designed to meet this challenge.

The international insertion of the region

Chapter VI

The fragility of the external context

In recent years, efforts by Latin American countries to advance their economic restructuring and development process have been hindered by the deterioration in the external environment, which has been undergoing a profound economic transition. This has set in motion adjustment processes and recessive cycles that have been accompanied by uncertainty and disruption. To comprehend, accept, and implement the changes that must be introduced into Latin America's development strategies, the profound transitions that took place on the international scene from 1950 to 1990 must be recognized.

Economic restructuring and the external context

In the early 1990s, international economic development was highly influenced by a series of economic, political, and military events that once again underscored the interdependence between these spheres. The first lesson that can be gleaned from this refers to the different perspective with which the great powers view the problems of the developed countries—be they the agenda of the Group of Seven, the reunification of Germany and the rapprochement of the two Europes, or the economic agreements within North America—and the problems of Latin America, to which they assign low priority. An initial conclusion that can be drawn from this is that, just as the problems of growth in the developed countries are approached within the context of these economic and political inter-relationships, there can be no cooperation for Latin American development without the adoption of the same perspective to bring the region's problems into focus.

Influence of recent events

The political forces unleashed in Eastern Europe beginning in 1989 set in motion a complex political transition not only from communist regimes to democratic systems of government but also from centrally-planned to market economies. This phenomenon once again corroborated the existence of an indissoluble link between political and economic processes. However, since the dismantling of the central planning system was not succeeded *pari passu* by the emergence of the conditions and institutions necessary to develop a market economy, the outcome in these countries was stagnation or a deterioration in the production of goods and services and in the distribution systems. The tensions and uncertainties in the Soviet Union as well as Yugoslavia, deriving from the age-old problem of diverse nationalities coexisting within the same political framework, aggravated these problems.

The crisis in the Persian Gulf cut oil production in Iraq, Jordan, and Kuwait virtually by half during the second part of 1990. Having a moderate effect on world economic development and adversely affecting growth in some countries, it served to remind us how vulnerable the world economy is to major political upheavals.

In Africa, in perhaps a quieter but nonetheless more dramatic way, a series of civil wars caused a widespread deterioration in the welfare level of the countries' populations, translating into terrible famines and relegating growth objectives to a secondary plane. Only in the Far East and South Asia did growth continue at rates similar to those of 1989, making this the region with the highest economic growth rate. In China, after the slowdown of 1989, the economy resumed an annual growth rate of 5 percent.

Negative trends in the world economy

The growth of the gross world product was once again very weak in 1991, prolonging a downturn in which it fell from 4.3 percent in 1988 to 3 percent in 1989 and 1 percent in 1990. Unemployment, which was significant in the developing countries—particularly Latin America—also became characteristic of the economies of Eastern Europe and the Soviet Union. By the late 1980s, the seven largest market economies, especially Canada, the United States, France, and the United Kingdom, entered a downturn for the first time since 1982, while Germany and Japan continued to grow, though at a slower rate. During the same period, average growth in the smaller industrialized economies also fell, although with considerable variations from country to country.[55]

In the early 1980s, inflation rose worldwide as a result of the increase in the price of oil and other raw materials. The industrialized nations reacted to this situation with restrictive monetary policies that constrained credit and raised interest rates, curbing economic growth and boosting unemployment. This new recessive cycle caused the GDP in the developed countries to fall by 0.3 percent in 1982. Their volume of exports fell by 1.2 percent, and their average price

---

[55] United Nations, *Informe económico mundial,* 1991; Word Bank, *Informe sobre el desarrollo mundial*, 1991; UNCTAD, *Trade and Development Report,* 1991; and CLEPI, *Informe sobre la economía mundial: perspectiva latinoamericana,* 1990-1991.

by about 5 percent. These trends drastically altered the terms of trade, to the detriment of the developing countries.

Monetary policy management has played an important role in the growth path of the industrialized countries since 1980. At that time, governments began to apply restrictive policies aimed at combatting rapid price increases and inflationary expectations through the contraction in demand. This allowed the countries to reduce their inflation from 12 percent in 1980 to no more than 4.6 percent between 1983 and 1990. During this time, the contraction in money supply was accompanied, naturally, by a significant rise in interest rates. In the latter years of the period, with inflationary expectations under control, money demand rose and the financial system was considerably deregulated. This led to the development of new financial instruments and operations that stimulated international liquidity and capital movement across borders. Part of this monetary movement was oriented toward the securities markets. The crisis in the New York Stock Exchange during the latter half of 1991 caused this trend to be reversed, and once more, restrictive monetary policies began to be applied. The European monetary system exhibited the same trend, following the anti-inflationary policy of the Bundesbank, notwithstanding some changes that this institution had recently introduced to facilitate the integration of the two Germanies.

Monetary and fiscal policies

This trend was even more pronounced in the case of Japan, in light of the rise in real estate and stock prices and the extraordinary expansion of the financial markets. As a consequence, in recent years, personal savings as a proportion of income fell drastically, while the ratio of debt to income rose substantially and corporate debt grew even more rapidly. The reduced capacity for credit absorption by individuals and corporations, lower real estate values, and other diverse factors began to sow doubts about the soundness of the financial system—particularly that of the United States, not only with regard to the savings and loan sector but to banks as well.

In recent years, the fiscal policy of the industrialized countries has reinforced these tendencies. Economic thought has traditionally recommended that governments increase spending or lower taxes during recessionary periods to stimulate aggregate demand, with the aim of re-establishing economic growth and generating employment. Conceptually, such measures should be adopted in conjunction with expansive monetary policies. Today, faced with the same situation, very few would recommend resorting to fiscal policy. In November 1991, after the temporary downturn in the New York Stock Exchange, *The Economist* predicted that both experts and the public would demand that the government do something to overcome the crisis. The article added that "this demand is a trap and constitutes the greatest danger that could occur in the event of a contraction in the market."[56]

One of the reasons for this attitude is the persistence of inflationary fears. Another is the discovery that fiscal policy is not always sufficient to fine tune the growth process in the short term: modifications in public spending and the tax system take too long, and there is the danger that the fiscal stimulus will make its appearance only after the recovery has commenced, with destabilizing effects on the process. Budgetary and tax policies appear to be more suitable for promoting specific programs in the medium term than for generating an overall stimulus to the economy, unless costs of this boost are ignored or the policy is implemented under extreme conditions. A third reason is that the room to maneuver for this type of policy is inversely proportional to the magnitude of the country's fiscal deficit, which is generally high in the industrialized nations—especially the United States, whose federal deficit bordered on $320 billion in 1991.

Differences in growth rates

The deceleration in the growth of the developed market economies since the 1980s has combined with increasingly divergent economic behavior among them. A clear indicator of this is the contrast between the policy of the Federal Reserve Board in the United States, and that of monetary authorities in Germany and Japan. Faced with recession in 1990, the Federal Reserve began to relax its monetary policy, with a consequent drop in interest rates. Germany and Japan, on the other hand, maintained a more dynamic growth process and high interest rates.

During this period, there was a strict correlation between the growth of trade and the gross domestic product. According to UNCTAD, although trade continued to grow at a rate almost double that of world production, its growth of 4.3 percent in 1990 and 3 percent in 1991 was in contrast to an annual rate of 6 percent during the 1985-1990 period. "Although trade has been defined as the engine of economic growth, the resulting damage from the current situation has worked in both directions: the recession in numerous developed countries in 1990 was one of the negative influences on international trade throughout that year."[57]

In sum, since the late 1980s, the international economic scene has been characterized by recessive tendencies, scant GDP

---

[56] *The Economist,* November 23, 1991.
[57] UNCTAD, *Trade and Development Report,* 1991.

growth, and a rise in unemployment—a situation that has been highly influenced by financial and fiscal variables. In recent years, uncertainty in the financial markets has grown with respect to interest rates, exchange rates, and share prices. Thus, on the one hand, there is the question of the extent to which the economies of the industrialized countries can be protected from the financial disturbances mentioned earlier. On the other, there is the question of how much the slowdown in growth derives from the shrinkage in some components of domestic demand, such as consumption and private investment. The slow growth in the gross world product and trade and the instability and uncertainty in the financial and foreign exchange markets provide a very unfavorable climate for Latin American economic growth—especially for the success of the structural reforms that these countries are attempting to implement.

An unfavorable external market

The world economic transition

Both the gradual nature of historical processes and their unpredictability make it difficult to appreciate the differences between our own era and the period when traditional Latin American economic thought developed. Between 1950 and 1990, we moved from a bipolar world to one that is irreversibly multipolar; from a world dominated by military security concerns to one where economic, social, and cultural considerations prevail; from an economic and technological paradigm with its roots in the last century to one that is profoundly transforming productive structures, societal organization, enterprises, grassroots communities, communications media, values, and people's perspectives. Participation by the various regions of the world in these transformations is extremely uneven, but the force with which transnationalization has advanced in today's world makes it imperative for all societies to face up to these changes and either eliminate or reduce the likelihood of embarking on development paths that are radically divergent or isolated.

1950-1990: Major transformations

In 1950, the world was dominated by the extraordinary economic and political power of the United States. This nation accounted for about 40 percent of world production. It was the only industrialized country that did not have problems related to the balance of payments or import restrictions. It possessed a technological base that was intact and highly modernized as a result of the war effort, and it produced the bulk of technological innovations and

Relative decline in the U.S. position

Nobelists in science. The United States was at the forefront in virtually every branch of industry, including areas traditionally dominated by European countries, such as the chemical, pharmaceutical, and capital goods industries, and its currency served as a universal medium of exchange. At the same time, direct foreign investment by the United States was considerably larger than the combined foreign investment of all the companies based in the rest of the world, thus setting in motion the expansion of the transnational corporation. Thanks to a high degree of domestic consensus and an acceptance of U.S. leadership, the country's economic vitality could be expressed in a manner that proved to be very positive for the international community, through such efforts as the Marshall Plan for Europe and the Point IV Program, which introduced assistance for the developing countries. Forty years later, U.S. production accounted for just 27 percent of world production. By 1990, the country's exports had fallen from 20 percent of global exports at the start of the period to 10 percent, and foreign investments by European and Japanese-based enterprises were three times those of the United States.

These shifts in the relative ranking of the United States in the world economy were accompanied by a marked reversal in its balance of payments positon. By 1990, the large positive balances in its current account and the massive transfers of capital destined for foreign investment had been replaced by major current account deficits and rising imports of capital to finance the national debt and industrial investment. This fueled concerns in certain quarters that if this trend were to continue for a number of years, the burden of the commitments associated with debt service payments could increase to the point of jeopardizing U.S. economic growth.

Profound forces were behind this trend. First, there was the loss of U.S. leadership in the area of technological changes that have a substantial impact on industrial transformation—with the exception of some sectors at the cutting edge of scientific development. This was followed by a relative slowdown in the growth of productivity in the country vis-à-vis other nations like Germany and Japan. Another factor was the move from self-sufficiency with respect to oil in 1950 to a situation in 1990 where half of the country's oil needs were imported. Moreover, the magnitude of the resources committed to social security programs must also be considered, for they came to drastically affect the size of the U.S. fiscal deficit. The rise in military spending over the past 30 years also contributed decisively to this phenomenon. One of its consequences was that the country's national debt rose from $747 billion to $2.4 trillion during the past decade, and from 29 percent to 45 percent of GDP during the same period.

The counterpart to the loss of the U.S. position has been the structural transformations in the world economy and geographical shifts or adjustments in the leadership exercised by the principal world economic centers or blocs.

After the 25 years of unprecedented expansion that characterized the postwar period, the world economy entered a long cycle of recession or turbulence. My interpretation of these events is that the world is witnessing a period of transformation, not stagnation, and moreover, that this transition is not something unprecedented, but may very well correspond to the theory of long-term economic cycles described by Kondradieff in 1935. The Russian economist did not systematically specify which factors explain the phases of boom and bust that characterize the world economic cycle, but among them may be demographic trends, the economic incorporation of new natural resources, technological innovations, and improvements in enterprise management, as well as political processes, wars, and revolutions. Prior to publishing his work, Kondradieff had managed to identify three such cycles, without witnessing the completion of the third. The projection of his line of analysis could lead to the conclusion that we are in the descending phase of a fourth cycle, a hypothesis that would provide material for an interesting historical academic analysis.[58]

A long cycle of recession and upheaval

All indications are that the world economy is in the middle of one of these structural transformation processes, and while its causes are extremely complex, three factors can be identified that have had—or will have—a major impact on the transition currently underway.

The first of these is the transnationalization of the world economy, which accelerated in the mid-1960s. This process was initially attributed to the rise of the transnational corporation, regarded as a new form of business activity and enterprise organization. At the time, the danger of "the American challenge" represented by the transnational corporation was being denounced in France, while in the United States, the old concept of national sovereignty was

The process of transnationalization

---

[58] N. Kondratieff, "The Long Waves in Economic Life," *Review of Economic Statistics,* November 1935; J.A. Schumpeter, *The Theory of Economic Development,* 1934; and F. Braudel, *Civilisation Matérielle, Economie at Capitalisme,* Vol. III, 1979. More recently, M. Olson analyzed the impact of the increase in corporate pressures on the economic cycle in *The Rise and Decline of Nations,* (op. cit.), and P. Kennedy, the links between war and economic growth through technological change in *The Rise and Fall of the Great Powers,* Random House, 1987.

being depicted as virtually corralled by these new types of enterprises.[59] With today's perspective, we can better appreciate that it was not the multinational corporation that unleashed this process. Rather, this type of organization was born in response to the transnationalization of production, trade, finance, consumption, and communications.[60]

In its economic manifestations, this process followed a trajectory that commenced with the expansion of world trade, continued with the internationalization of the productive cycle, and culminated in the transnationalization of finance. This phenomenon may be due to the development of production technologies and forms of enterprise organization that permitted the division of productive processes, integrated them more fully into the markets, and made these processes more flexible, enabling them to offer a growing variety of goods and services produced in an increasingly decentralized manner.

This trend was fostered by the revolution in the fluidity, versatility and cost of transportation and communications. Transportation costs have fallen to one-quarter and communications to one-twentieth of what they were in 1950. The postwar drive toward the liberalization of international trade and the more recent trend toward the deregulation of the markets, with some exceptions, have contributed powerfully to stimulating this process. One measure of this has been the more rapid growth of intra-firm or intra-sectoral trade, consisting of commerce in manufactures within the same product line, in comparison with the growth in intersectoral trade—without taking into account the fact that over the past 40 years, trade has grown faster than world production.

All this has profoundly altered many ideas that held sway over the economic process, both worldwide and in Latin America. Comparative advantage has been redefined as a much more dynamic element than in the past. Such advantages have come to depend far less on labor and natural resources. The market, the design, and the manufacture of products have been integrated, making productive structures extraordinarily flexible. Trade is no longer dominated by the exchange of complementary products—such as raw materials for

---

[59] J. J. Servan-Schreiber, *Le Défie Américaine,* 1966, and R. Vernon, *Sovereignty at Bay: The Multilateral Spread of U.S. Enterprises,* New York, Basic Books, 1968.

[60] L. Tomassini, ed., *El Proceso de transnacionalización y el desarrollo de los países latinoamericanos,* Buenos Aires, GEL, 1986, and *La política internacional en un mundo posmoderno,* Buenos Aires, GEL, 1991.

manufactured goods—instead, it is concentrated in commerce pertaining to the same sector. The weight of services in production and international trade has increased. The mobility of the factors of production has grown, and the role of foreign investment has become more important, especially in developing countries.

To fully develop these characteristics, it has been necessary to strengthen the intersectoral integration of the national economies, in recognition of the systemic nature of these transformations. There has also been greater integration among the State, the market, and the private sector, while government economic policies have been obliged to take corporate strategies much more into account. Likewise, it has been necessary to make an effort to reconcile economic policies with apparently different objectives—policies in the areas of trade, industry, technology, and human resource development—to raise the global competitiveness of the economy, and to adapt domestic policies much more to those of other national players or to global economic trends.

Another factor that accounts for the transition underway in the world economy and the process of transnationalization itself is technological change. The changes that have occurred over the past two decades have been so profound that there has been talk of a "third industrial revolution."[61] Technological change is produced incrementally, through gradual improvements in certain processes or products; through radical change, via the introduction of completely new elements; or even through modifications with the potential to transform the entire productive system, leading to a new technological paradigm. This paradigm represents a constellation of interrelated technical and economic innovations that affect most branches of the productive apparatus.

Technological transformation

Any new technological paradigm has a key element, a common denominator or a dialectic that permeates the whole of the productive system. This common denominator could be coal, the steam engine, and the railroad during the first half of the nineteenth century, steel and electricity during the second, and oil, the internal combustion engine, petrochemicals, and the assembly line in the twentieth century. The key factors behind any new technological system must possess certain characteristics: for example, they must be low-cost, be in abundant or practically unlimited supply, have a wide variety of applications, and be suitable for incorporation into the foundation of numerous technological chains that, in turn, generate

---

[61] C. Ominami, ed., op. cit.

other product lines. Today, that common denominator would appear to be microelectronics and information technology.

The intensive use of these elements has given rise to new types of productive plants, marketing mechanisms, and financial systems. It has increased plant flexibility and product diversity, fostered enterprise decentralization and integration, given rise to new forms of urban and community organization, and even generated types of offices and households whose functions are carried out more efficiently with the help of information. The utilization of these technologies has brought the demand, design, production, and marketing of products more closely together and permitted a much more flexible and rapid response to market signals. It has also allowed the players in the productive process to multiply and, of course, has made them more competitive. The improvement in the developing countries' international competitiveness, though oriented toward less sophisticated activities than in the industrialized nations and toward small niches in the market, presupposes the incorporation of these technological changes.

Changes at the enterprise level are another factor that has influenced the transformation of the world economy. New technologies, improvements in transportation and communications, and the intensive use of information in the productive processes has encouraged the advance of transnationalization and facilitated the establishment of enterprise branches abroad or the disaggregation of their productive activities. These changes have favored the adoption of more decentralized and flexible organizational models, while maintaining communication between the different units, as well as a certain degree of central control. The adoption of a modern organizational structure for enterprises is as crucial from the standpoint of economic growth as the incorporation of technological innovation. Moreover, the new forms of organization and management constitute technology in themselves and are an integral part of a systemic process of technological change. Adopting these organizational innovations allows modern management methods to be applied not just to existing enterprises, but to new firms at the cutting edge of the productive system and to small as well as large enterprises. Such innovations also make it possible to extend these systems to nonprofit activities, such as health care services and education, raising their efficiency levels and lowering costs. Above all, they facilitate technological innovation itself.

The new paradigm that is emerging in the world economy is characterized by new concepts of efficiency for organizing production at the factory level, new models of management and enterprise

*New forms
of enterprise
organization*

structure, and less work per unit of product, with higher quality control. It also includes a strong bias in favor of the intensive use of the elements common to the new technological paradigm, new patterns of investment centered on sectors that make intensive use of those elements (and thus, new profiles in the composition of what is produced), a redefinition of the optimum scale of production, and new geographical patterns of investment and forms of linkage between the different units of the modernized productive networks. The key characteristic of the new enterprise organization is its ability to respond flexibly to the demands of the economic and social environment in which it functions.

Drucker identifies seven sources of innovation at the enterprise level, some endogenous and some exogenous. These include unforeseen events; differences between reality and assumptions by enterprises; innovations demanded by the application of a given productive process; changes in the structure of a branch of industry or the market; new technological know-how; changes in public perceptions, values, and preferences; and demographic transformations.[62] When faced with these trends, Latin American countries confront not only the challenge of achieving a better balance between State and private sector activity, but also of promoting the adoption of new forms of enterprise organization.

The transformation of the former Soviet Union, the reforms in Eastern Europe, and the end of the Cold War will profoundly alter the stimuli and the parameters that have influenced the evolution of the world economy for the past 40 years. Throughout the postwar period, the military-industrial complex was considered a highly important factor in technological change and world economic growth, especially as a result of the Cold War. Today, this trend has changed. The great powers have come to realize that defense expenditures constitute a heavy burden on their economies. The huge difference in defense spending between Japan and the Soviet Union during the postwar years accounts to a large extent for the rise of Japan and the profound economic transformations that the Soviet Union is being forced to undergo.

A new view of defense spending

Along with these structural features, the world economic transition has geographical aspects that are both interesting and a cause for concern among the Latin American countries. The growing geographical dispersion of the centers of growth and technological innovation and their constant change, derived from the divergent

Economic situations on the geographical level

---

[62] P. F. Drucker, *Innovation and Entrepreneurship*, Harper and Row, 1985.

rates of increase in productivity among the different countries and sectors, continually alter the regional structure of the new international political economy. Three facts have become fundamentally important from a geographical standpoint. First, the end of the Cold War will diminish the relevance of interests linked with strategic security and will give primacy to economic interests—an area where the United States will have a less relevant but equally significant role than in the past. Second, progress toward European unity and economic reforms in the former Soviet republics and Eastern Europe will give the Old World a new role, though it is impossible to predict whether it will be linked with a protectionist tendency or help to stimulate world economic growth. Third, Japan will continue as the world's largest creditor and the preeminent leader in technology, with production surpassing three-quarters that of the United States by the year 2000. "The Big Three of economics will supplant the Big Two of nuclear competition as the powers that will shape much of the 21st Century."[63]

New forms of insertion by the Latin American countries

In this context, the external interests of the developing countries in general and the Latin American countries in particular, and the way they insert themselves into the international markets, face great transformations. During the postwar period, primarily the 1950s and 1960s, the countries of the region followed an inward-oriented growth strategy. On the external front, this strategy attempted to bridge the double gap of trade and savings, defending the prices of these nations' main export products—composed largely of primary goods—and attempting to secure external resources under concessional terms. In the medium and long term, industrialization emerged as the only process capable of altering the countries' status as exporters of raw materials and of modifying the most unfavorable aspects of the relationship between the center and the periphery. At that time, stabilizing the price of basic products and obtaining external aid needed to be based on cooperation with the industrialized countries.

The early 1970s were characterized by a complex combination of progress and failure; of popular discontent and changes in direction by the political regimes in the region that had pursued this strategy; a growing decline in support for development cooperation in the majority of the industrialized countries; the independence of over a hundred developing nations as a result of the decolonization process; and, after 1973, the mounting power of the OPEC coun-

---

[63] C.F. Bergsten, "The World Economy after the Cold War," in *Foreign Affairs,* Vol. 69, No 3, Summer 1990.

tries—and vicariously, the rest of the developing world. These circumstances led developing countries to embark on a strategy that propounded the establishment of a new international economic order through the creation of global mechanisms for the defense of basic commodities prices, automatic concessional aid with appropriate increases, the industrialization of the developing countries, and the control of the activities of multinational corporations and the process of technology transfer—objectives debated for several years under the aegis of what has been termed the North-South dialogue. This dialogue ended in 1980 after the final round of "global negotiations" and was followed two years later by the debt crisis.

What had happened was that, while formally participating in the North-South dialogue, Latin American and other developing nations had attempted to soften the impact of the rise in oil prices and the international recession and keep on growing. They did so by recurring to external indebtedness, made possible for the first time since the Great Depression of the 1930s (though under very different circumstances) by the rebirth of international financial markets characterized by the increase in the debt with the private banks. This opened the door to a decade of painful adjustments in the debtor nations. The rest of this story is recounted in another chapter.

The international insertion strategy of the Latin American countries must respond both to the current international situation and to the changes that they are attempting to introduce into their economies. We live in an increasingly transnational and interdependent world, where productive structures are undergoing profound transformations under the force of powerful technological changes and new forms of enterprise organization, and where national and regional players—the new economic blocs—are multiplying and acting ever more competitively. The initial stages of the adjustment policies behind them, the Latin American countries one by one are trying to move beyond macroeconomic equilibria and introduce structural reforms into their productive apparatus, embrace modern technologies, integrate their economies and make them flexible and open, and increasingly penetrate the international markets. The idea that the ties between the economies of the developing countries and the industrialized nations can be severed and that countries can opt for a separate development path is not viable in today's world nor is it compatible with the interests of Latin America's governments.

What is most noticeable about the outward-oriented productive restructuring strategies that the majority of the region's countries are embarking upon is their more realistic and better informed perception about the nature of the present international context and

Productive restructuring and penetration of the world markets

133

the need to make their productive systems and development strategies compatible with it. In this vein, Latin America's economic leaders have come to realize that it is impossible to separate domestic economic policies from international economic developments.

Thus, a new strategy of greater international insertion presupposes domestic transformations, principally on two levels: the macroeconomic level, through the effective application of stabilization policies and the re-establishment of the respective equilibria, without which an economy cannot project itself energetically and continuously in the international markets, nor even collaborate fruitfully in a regional or subregional market; and the structural level, on which this new strategy presupposes the introduction of structural reforms in the countries' productive, financial, and marketing systems, which may imply reforms in monetary, tax, fiscal and trade policies, in industrialization and technological development strategies, and in human resource development efforts.

Latin America's postwar development pattern was based on the assumption that the public and private spheres were separate, the enterprise sector very weak, and that promoting development was basically the responsibility of the State. Forty years later, this situation has changed: economic players have proliferated; we look much more to the private sector for initiatives and financing; and new forms of interaction between the State, the enterprise sector, and the markets are becoming necessary.

Recent developments in the integration processes

Finally, four processes currently underway to support a vigorous insertion of the Latin American countries into the international economy are worth mentioning. The first is the recent evolution of integration in Latin America. It is well known that the traditional Latin American integration schemes established early in the 1960s long ago entered a state of paralysis or exhaustion. However, in the past decade, new integration initiatives have emerged with characteristics very different from those of the past and with greater probabilities of success. In 1986, an integration agreement signed by Argentina and Brazil began a movement toward economic unity between the two countries by the year 2000. The protocols that accompanied that decision included a markedly sectoral agreement. Among their positive features were the breadth and novelty of the sectoral spectrum and the fact that many of the sectors involved were on the cutting edge of the development process in both countries.

The 1990 agreement between the presidents of Argentina and Brazil in Buenos Aires pushed the goal of a common market forward to 1995 and added to the sectoral elements a progressive, automatic, and linear program of reciprocal across-the-board tariff reductions. This process served as one of the precedents for another initiative in 1990 between Argentina, Brazil, Paraguay, and Uruguay, aimed at creating a Southern Cone Common Market, or MERCOSUR, which includes a program of automatic tariff reductions to be completed one year after that of Argentina and Brazil, the adoption of a common external tariff, the complete liberalization of the movement of goods and factors of production, and the reconciliation of macroeconomic policies to ensure equal conditions for competition in trade. The Government of Chile, for its part, has entered into bilateral free trade agreements with Argentina, Mexico, Venezuela, and the United States. Colombia, Mexico, and Venezuela, in turn, have signed an economic complementation agreement, forming the "Group of Three."

In the face of these events, in late 1990, the Rio Group, meeting in Caracas, decided to undertake an evaluation of LAIA, in order to endow it with the flexibility and efficiency demanded by today's circumstances and to examine its compatibility with the trade situation, both inside and outside the region. Several presidential summits have attempted to infuse the Andean Group with a new vitality that will permit evolution toward a new community of nations modeled after the European Community, and include economic policy coordination, the adoption of joint industrial and trade policies, and cooperation in energy, agriculture, and social and cultural areas. Major initiatives have also been underway to reactivate both the Central American Common Market, whose operations have been interrupted by a number of political and military conflicts, and the Caribbean Community (CARICOM).

What is interesting are the new features of these intitiatives. First, the majority of these efforts are grounded in the assumption that what allows integration to take place is the economic behavior of the countries that are integrating—their stability and vitality—and not simply their degree of economic complementarity or their geographical proximity, as evidenced by agreements between distant countries. Second, as a corollary to this idea, these programs presuppose the coordination of macroeconomic, industrial, and trade policies. Third, nearly all of the initiatives tend to combine traditional trade liberalization measures with sectoral programs aimed at increasing competitiveness and bringing about productive restructuring. None of them have been designed to protect an expanded market from international competition. Rather, they are grounded precisely in the assumption of a high degree of shared competitiveness. Finally, and for this reason, these are integration agreements oriented more toward the international markets than toward past experiences.

Another element, with seemingly ambiguous consequences, is the trend toward the formation of large regional economic blocs that revolve around the three major groups mentioned earlier. These blocs represent a pragmatic response to the erosion that has taken place in the movement toward trade liberalization. There is no clear answer to the question of whether we are faced with the establishment of these trade blocs. What is clear are the factors that have fostered this trend, such as the erosion of the GATT, the new forms of protectionism and managed trade, and the fruitless efforts of the United States to launch a new round of trade negotiations early in the last decade—efforts that have met with resistance over the topics of agriculture and services prior to the start of the Uruguay Round. "At present," warns the GATT, "world markets are not opening up: they are under pressure from a growing tide of restrictions. Demands for greater protection are heard in every country, and from one branch of industry to another."[64]

In addition, the nature and orientation of the three economic blocs that appear to be forming are very different. Of course, U.S. and Canadian motives for entering into a free trade agreement were also different: the United States intended to serve notice to the international community that it could take similar bilateral action if some members continued to oppose a new round of multilateral trade negotiations, while Canada wanted to make provisions in the face of growing U.S. protectionism. Moreover, this agreement is not as far-reaching as the one that will establish a single European market, beginning in 1992, when the European Community transforms itself from a tariff union with a common external tariff to an integrated Europe that will embrace not only trade liberalization but the free circulation of capital and labor and a high degree of harmonization of the countries' macroeconomic policies. The consequences of this step with regard to the European Community's trade with the rest of the world are not clear, despite the reassuring message contained in the document issued by the commission in 1988, entitled "Europe 1992: Europe World Partner."

In contrast, the formation of a common economic sphere in the Asian Pacific—based on increased trade and investment, the synchronization of global adjustments and structural changes, and the appreciation of the yen—still appears to be compatible with a broad opening toward the world economy. In any case, there is no reason to seriously fear that these economic spheres will turn into

---

[64] GATT, Wisemen's Report, *Trade Policies for a Better Future.*

closed blocs and fragment the international economy; the danger is that the greater activity inside these blocs will accentuate the peripheral footing of Latin American countries or further limit their options, causing them once again to look exclusively to the United States. The response to this danger should come from an endogenous effort by the countries of the region to restructure their economies, increase their competitiveness, and continue to fight tenaciously to gain access to other markets.

The Enterprise for the Americas Initiative falls auspiciously within these trends. In 1989, th U.S.-Canada agreement to establish a free trade zone between the two countries over a 10-year period went into effect, and in 1991, negotiations commenced to extend this zone to Mexico. Broadening it to include the entire hemisphere "from Alaska to Tierra del Fuego" is the long-term objective of the Initiative launched by the President of the United States. To reach this goal, the government of that country has already established basic bilateral agreements with the majority of the countries in Latin America, as well as with the CARICOM and MERCOSUR groups. In each of these agreements, the principles that shall govern specific accords in the future are defined and an agency is established with a mixed composition, generally called the Council on Trade and Investment.

The Enterprise for the Americas Initiative has three main components: mechanisms to reduce the external debt of the Latin American countries, linked with programs to protect the environment; the possibility of establishing trade liberalization programs; and the promotion of investments within the hemisphere. This latter component refers not only to measures aimed at attracting foreign investment to the countries of the area, but also at rebuilding confidence among national investors to encourage them to keep their investments in the country or bring back expatriated capital. This trend, of course, presupposes profound economic reforms and the adoption of policies that allow market forces to operate, attracting such investment. The investment component of the Enterprise of the Americas Initiative has been placed in the hands of the Inter-American Development Bank. To this end, as we have noted, a Multilateral Investment Fund has been created to provide technical assistance and support for private enterprise and for programs for human resource development.

Response of the Enterprise for the Americas Initiative

Another element is the troubled trajectory of the Uruguay Round and the GATT. Opened in September 1986, with the intent of concluding in 1990, the Uruguay Round had a more ambitious scope than its predecessors. While major tariff reductions had been won, there were still significant barriers with regard to some sectors and

Trade negotiations

products. Indeed, even in the 1980s a certain resurgence of protectionism in the developed countries was seen, chiefly in sectors suffering the consequences of the greater competitiveness of the world economy. These measures were primarily of the nontariff type, consisting essentially of anti-dumping measures, compensatory duties, and voluntary limitations on certain types of exports—which were being used as discriminatory tools, undermining the norms of the GATT. The purpose of the Uruguay Round was to impose discipline on these practices and bring about greater tariff liberalization. Its agenda, however, went much further, covering such areas as the service sector, intellectual property, and foreign investment. In addition to these issues were the old problems created by the agricultural trade policy of some of the industrialized countries, particularly those of the European Community.

This round of negotiations was not satisfactorily concluded during the time allotted and was extended through 1991, finally achieving positive results that will permit a major reversal of protectionist tendencies, a renewal of the trade liberalization process, more effective governance of the existing multilateral mechanisms, the application of clearer "rules of the game" and mechanisms that recognize differences in development between parties, according special treatment to weaker countries—particularly in the new areas of services, intellectual property rights, and foreign investment. The achievements of late 1991 are the start of a response to the pressing need to compensate the efforts of Latin American countries to restructure their economies and open them more to the international markets, and they are consistent with the advancement of trade liberalization on a global level.

The need for economic convergence

Greater international insertion by the Latin American countries and the internal reforms that it demands presuppose a requirement that historically has been very difficult to attain in the region: a certain degree of convergence in economic thought that goes beyond peaceful coexistence among the different schools. The painful lessons of the lost decade and the rich experiences of the silent transformation that, transcending adjustment, many Latin American countries have already begun, have permitted progress in this direction after long decades of conflict among the various ideologies. In the external context, this trend is consistent with the globalization of the world economy and the spread of a new technological paradigm, and in the political sphere, with the end of the East-West struggle and therefore the disappearance of these two conflicting models. If we closely observe the evolution of the world economy in this century, we find that perhaps the greatest difference between the economic systems of the Western world and the socialist systems was the greater openness of the former to adaptation and change. The social market economies of today, based on the diffusion of technology and entirely new forms of organization, have very little in common with the economies of the railroad, steel, or assembly line production of earlier periods. The paralysis and ultimate fall of the Soviet model does not represent the end of history. To sustain this argument would mean an acceptance that the engine of history is not innovation but conflict.

International economic coordination

World economic development has witnessed two periods of stability and growth based on the existence of clear "rules of the game" and the orderly application of these rules. In both cases, these conditions developed under the shadow of a great power that exerted its political and economic hegemony throughout the world. The first was the era dominated by Great Britain and the pound sterling, from the second half of the nineteenth century to World War I; the second, the postwar period following World War II, characterized by the overwhelming supremacy of the United States and the U.S. dollar. There has been much debate as to whether the presence of a hegemonic power is a prerequisite for maintaining a world economic order.[65] However, since politics is the art of the possible—and this applies to international politics as well—it seems more realistic to ponder whether the restoration of this type of hegemony, particularly that of the United States, is viable in today's world. In a world economy tending toward fragmentation—not only among the three great centers mentioned earlier, but among other smaller but highly efficient industrialized nations, a growing group of newly-industrialized countries that are aggressively penetrating world markets, oil-exporting countries, and the great economic and demographic powers of the future, such as India and China—the answer appears to be no. Therefore, the question is, what course can be adopted to manage the world economy in a fragmented world?

Periods dominated by an economic center

[65] See S. Strange, *Sterling-Dollar Diplomacy,* 1980; R. Gilpin, *Political Economy of International Relations,* 1987; and R. Keohane, *Beyond Hegemony,* 1988.

In an age characterized by major upheavals, finding an answer to this question becomes extremely urgent. Indeed, the economic headlines in the newspapers of the 1950s and 1960s were few and reassuring: in the industrialized countries, exchange rates and interest rates varied little, inflation was low, and trade and financial flows were dynamic and stable. From the mid-1970s through the 1980s, however, the front pages began to be dominated by alarming headlines about the magnitude of fiscal deficits, interest rate fluctuations, the volatility of exchange rates, trade wars, the countries' external debt, and the fragility of the international financial system. These marked disturbances, naturally, were an expression of the structural transformations just mentioned. The structure of production in the majority of the countries and its technological base have been profoundly altered; international trade has continued to expand, and its structure has changed; and controls on the international capital markets have diminished and many national financial institutions have been deregulated. The industrialized countries are far more interdependent than before. However, the political structures that provide the framework for these processes and the authorities that manage them have not altered their nature, and they continue to operate from a national perspective. Authorities charged with the formulation of economic policy in the various countries are faced with the challenge of having to coordinate their policies ever more closely with those of other nations. To respond to the question of how to manage the international economy without the presence of a hegemonic power, it is once more appropriate not only to consider abstract options but to observe reality. In recent years, this reality shows the development of very interesting, though still inadequate, efforts at coordinating the policies of the principal players in the world economy.

In a world where the transmission of economic phenomena generates growing interdependence, it is impossible to allow the economic policies of the great centers to be passed on without a minimum of consensus and coordination of national policies. The erosion of national autonomy can lead to diverse types of relationships that range from open conflict, at one end of the spectrum, to complete economic integration, at the other. Before arriving at this latter stage—which is very difficult to achieve—many countries have experimented with various forms of economic cooperation, including policy coordination.

This is a process wherein the countries attempt to reconcile their respective economic policies—which often implies modifying them—in recognition of a situation of growing interdependence and in order to create a more stable, predictable, and favorable international economic environment. The seriousness of this process can be measured by the magnitude of the changes that the participating countries are willing to introduce into their economic policies. There has been much discussion as to whether this process tends to usurp national autonomy. While the countries' need to introduce changes to adapt their policies to those of other countries may infringe on their autonomy, it is no less true that such coordination broadens a country's options, providing it with a measure of control over the policies of others.

In recent decades, there have been interesting developments in this respect—especially at the level of regional groupings—from the policy coordination process within the European Community to the coordinating and consultative forums established by the Latin American countries, primarily within the framework of LAES and later, at the Rio Group. Undoubtedly, however, the development with the greatest global impact has been the formation of the Group of Seven. Based on earlier precedents and, more specifically, following the Plaza Agreement in September 1985, the seven largest economies in the world adopted an extremely flexible multilateral system for coordinating and supervising their economic policies through summit meetings, with the participation of the ministries of the Treasury or Finance. Later these encounters began to coincide with the semiannual meetings of the International Monetary Fund's Interim Committee and the World Bank's Development Committee. Since this example is the closest we have to policy coordination in the world economy in the absence of a hegemonic power, it is useful to reflect briefly on the players, the proceedings, and the results of this experience up to now.

The informality and flexibility of these meetings exhibits both the advantages and disadvantages of this type of mechanism. From a substantive viewpoint, it seems appropriate to insist on the integration of efforts between the adjustment of exchange rates, on the one hand, and the coordination of macro and microeconomic policies, on the other; on the need to distinguish more clearly between emergency and medium-term measures, bolstering the identity and importance of the latter; and on incorporating into the agenda aspects that have hardly been touched upon until now, such as military spending or environmental preservation, perhaps because they have been considered to be noneconomic in nature. From an institutional standpoint, it is necessary, at the very least, to establish mechanisms for the collective memory, for cumulative analysis, and for the systematic follow-up of the consultations and agreements reached at

Flexibility with institutionalization

each meeting that can link them to one another and eventually lead to a new way of governing the world economy.

The conflict between the need to more actively incorporate institutions like the central banks, the financial sector, and representatives of other interests, and the need to keep these processes confined within a small circle must also be resolved. The automatic application of the agreements reached at these summit meetings and the links between these meetings and national administrations are probably the greatest issues pending on this front.

Participation by the developing countries

However, in recent decades, a profound conflict has materialized between progress toward interdependence and the management of world economic affairs from national decision making centers. In the event that it is feasible to continue developing projects to coordinate these policies, another contradiction will emerge between the management of this process by the larger economies and the need for other international players to participate in it. I have already pointed out that in the contemporary world economic scene, the great economic powers are competing and increasingly establishing ties not only with other industrialized countries with high levels of efficiency and technology, but also with a growing number of newly-industrialized nations, as well as with demographic or economic giants whose weight is already heavily felt or will be felt in the future. The lack of participation by other international players in this coordination process may have very serious economic and political repercussions. In a transnational world, industrial and technological competition, the creation and restructuring of trade loops, movements of financial and investment resources, political or labor migrations, and threats to environmental integrity may come from a wide variety of players. Objective mechanisms must be conceived to permit greater participation by all of them in this process.

Foundation for an economic agenda for the 1990s

Chapter VII

Background and objectives

The preceding chapters attempted to provide a historical overview of the various economic stages of Latin American development throughout its long journey toward economic growth and social justice. Reconciling economic efficiency with social justice is an old challenge for economic theory and a permanent objective of governments and their political leaders.

Economic growth and equity

We have witnessed efforts that have attempted to maximize efficiency and economic growth by stimulating the development of the productive forces—some relying on State action alone and others seeking an association between the State and private enterprise. When the emphasis has been solely on the economic aspect, neglecting the equity of the system, the result has been an economy without a society, fueling social conflict and political instability.

When efforts have concentrated on resolving social problems spurred by the region's grave economic disequilibria and the ethical demand for social justice, macroeconomic equilibria have been neglected; in most cases, the results have been a growth in populism and rampant inflation, stifling economic growth. In these cases, we have had society without economy.

In earlier chapters we highlighted the basic elements of the postwar economic model. We also analyzed the evolution of its crisis, exacerbated by the external debt incurred by the region during the 1970s.

The 1980s witnessed the outbreak of this model's crisis, and the reaction to it gave rise first to painful adjustments and then to a series of structural reforms that formed a more or less uniform policy prescription in nearly every country.

From recent history, one could surmise that, after the painful experiences of the crisis and the lessons learned outside the region, Latin America would comprehend better than ever the basic rules of economic growth. The following questions arise: Are these rules sufficient to solve the multiple problems confronting the region? Should a broadened agenda be put forward that deals with the two great issues that these rules must include? Internally, how can a social policy be designed that generates the equitable conditions fundamental to ensuring the social and political viability of the economic modernization process? Externally, can the region be vigorously reinserted into the world economy, based on greater competitiveness fostered by an intelligent economic modernization process?

These are indeed the objectives that should be included in a broadened agenda for the 1990s, around which an authentic "Latin American consensus" can be built.

The Latin American agenda

Once more, we reiterate that there is a better understanding today in all Latin American countries of the causes and nature of the crisis, as well as a growing awareness of the need to go beyond recessive economic adjustment policies and pursue other goals. To do so, ten objectives can serve as the underpinnings of an agenda for the design of the region's economic and social policies for the 1990s.

1. Ensure the economic viability of the modernization process and consolidate the reforms currently in progress.

2. Promote the social viability of this model through a frontal attack on poverty and the implementation of a social reform program that, with distributive equity, incorporates the most marginal segments of society into the productive process.

3. Reduce the size of the State by promoting reforms aimed at placing limits on its presence, while at the same time bolstering both its capacity to orient the development process and its efficiency in carrying out the tasks that are proper to it and cannot be renounced.

4. Strengthen the ability of private sector agents to operate, through the creation of a favorable investment climate.

5. Promote the incorporation of the most advanced technology into the productive processes in order to enhance the region's international competitiveness.

6. Undertake a massive and modern process of human resource development at all educational levels—a process compatible with the needs of the current economic model and with the achievement of distributive equity.

7. Intensify regional economic integration processes, strengthening their new characteristics aimed at promoting change in productive structures and improving the international competitiveness of the participating countries.

8. Define Latin America's new forms of insertion into the international market and its new modes of interaction with the region's traditional partners.

9. Ensure that the development model to be established is environmentally sustainable.

10. Consolidate democratic advances through the building of political consensus and improvements in the quality, professionalism, and transparency of public activities.

I would now like to refer briefly to the different elements of this economic agenda for the 1990s.

Economic viability and the consolidation of the reforms

The first requisite for the viability of this economic model is maintaining the basic economic equilibria to ensure that the price system functions properly in line with the normal operation of market forces. Many ruptures in these macroeconomic equilibria have stemmed from artificial and distortionary interventions in the price-setting mechanisms. Historically, however, the most distortionary element of all has been fiscal disequilibria at all levels—global, local, and in the public enterprise sector. The battle for fiscal equilibrium is now under way throughout the region, accompanied by painful adjustments in public expenditures and sustained efforts at improving income generation. This battle targets the very root of the profound inflationary disorders of the past decade, which inflicted such damage on Latin American economies and societies. The healthy recovery of public finances should be a priority of State reform.

Another element essential to economic dynamism is ensuring that the financial markets work correctly. This includes an appropriate balance between the deregulation and supervision of these markets, as well as the proper management of interest rates and greater efficiency among financial intermediaries. Financial reform is another requisite for the model's economic viability. A basic element of this reform should be an increasingly independent role for the central banks—something that is already occurring in some countries.

Domestic economic liberalization and openness to the international markets have gained a good deal of ground in the region and are beginning to be reflected in Latin America's improving competitiveness—not without great controversies and debate regarding the depth, extent and pace of the external opening. Indeed, trade reform is another major chapter in the process of improving the region's international competitiveness.

Liberalization and deregulation

The general deregulation of the economy is already incorporated into the economic rationale of our countries. Steps should be taken, nevertheless, to ensure that deregulation has limits and proceeds at a pace appropriate to the realities of each country. Its effectiveness, however, will always depend on the State's ability to orient it. Deregulation should liberate the energies of society and its economic agents. State supervision will prevent control by the few over the market mechanisms.

One of the basic challenges of the growth process is how to increase the level of savings and investment and channel these savings toward the productive sectors. The gap created by investments not made during the past decade—on the order of $70 billion annually—has constituted a powerful drag on the development process. Similarly, fiscal balance—in the State, public enterprises, and municipalities—is fundamental to increasing public investment and allocating it toward productive or social ends.

Creating a climate of confidence conducive to price stability ensures an increase in private savings and discourages the capital flight that has drained so many resources from their domestic productive function. New ways to finance social security systems have been adding considerable savings to the regional economy. The generation of domestic savings should go hand in hand with channeling them toward the productive sectors. In this task, the development of capital markets is essential. A climate of confidence created by economic stability and the incentive of an environment favorable to investment—both domestic and foreign—will facilitate capital repatriation, promote direct foreign investment, and make possible the region's return to the international credit markets.

The social viability of the model

We have stressed that macroeconomic equilibria are a necessary but not sufficient condition for ensuring the social efficiency of the model. Latin America has contracted an enormous social debt with its peoples—a debt with roots in the region's historical inheritance and one which the development strategies applied in recent decades have not been able to liquidate. This social debt drastically increased during the 1980s, owing to the economic crisis and the implementation of adjustment programs that in many cases inevitably exacerbated conditions of social exclusion and extreme poverty.

We have maintained that beyond theoretical controversies, the correction of social imbalances will not be achieved solely through the proper functioning of market forces. It will require public policies and a strong commitment on the part of leaders, governments, and societies in general. This does not preclude, however, the mobilization of private sector agents and market mechanisms. Given the magnitude of the social problem, supporting the private sector in areas like education, health, housing, and social security cannot be ruled out, and there are rich and innovative experiences of this type that the State can attempt to reproduce.

The State's commitment to the social question should be grounded in strengthening its financial stability and improving its capacity to intervene through social investment. This makes effective State intervention in social questions essentially dependent on its success on two fronts: mobilizing fiscal resources and improving the quality of public expenditures in the social sectors. Moreover, the increase in the tax burden and the improvement in tax collection reinforce one another. The State will have no capacity for social intervention without fiscal resources, and *that* is linked to tax payment and collection. In carrying out these functions, there is also the problem of equity in the distribution of the tax burden. Fiscal reform should aim at distributive justice.

Social role of the State

Hand in hand with greater fiscal revenue should go an improvement in the quality of public expenditures. History shows that the basic problem is not *more* but rather *better* spending. The quality of public outlays is thus an essential component of the State's ability to intervene in social problems. Unproductive expenditures, bureaucracy, and above all in today's world, excessive military spending, constrain its action.

The State's capacity for efficient intervention in the social question should be evidenced in several areas:

a) One concerns preferential treatment in situations of extreme poverty through policies aimed at transferring resources to sectors most in need. These actions have became indispensable and urgent within the framework of the adjustment programs, pointing to the need for job creation and maintaining minimal standards in the fields of health, urban renewal, education, housing, etc. This requires a redefinition of objectives, in addition to institutional reforms, new legal and regulatory mechanisms, and of course, new investment resources.

Social policies

b) Another basic area of action consists of support to the informal sector of the economy, with a view toward stimulating small entrepreneurs and informal sector workers, either to improve the productivity of their activities, or to promote their transfer to more highly productive activities that lead to higher employment and income and social mobility. In recent years, Latin America's informal sector has acquired enormous importance; since the second half of the 1980s, the number of persons employed in this sector is estimated to have increased by more than 50 percent. Hence, based on plausible estimates, some 30 percent of the product today is being generated in the informal sector. In the past, this sector was defined essentially as a hidden pocket of unemployment or unproductive work and thus, a social problem waiting to be solved. Today, on the contrary, it is considered development potential that should be stimulated through institutional reforms, human resource development, a more flexible productive and financial mechanism, and sufficient allocation of resources toward these ends.

c) Another area includes the definition and promotion of population policies linked with the demographic pressures still present in many countries of the region. In this context, the problems of specific groups stand out—problems related to the demographic pyramid and to the opportunity of certain age groups to participate in the development process. The problems of infants, of youth and women entering the job market, and the enhancement of social security for the elderly have taken on great significance and urgency.

State reform

The debate surrounding the role of the State in society in general and in the economy in particular is not a new one in Latin America or the rest of the world. However, the adoption of an economic model based more than ever on the role of the market and private enterprise as the protagonists of development has caused this debate to be couched in new terms.

The market and the role of the State

We must begin by recognizing that we have no unique formula regarding the structure and functions of the State that corresponds to an economy more strongly influenced by market forces. We know that the role of the State has been significant, and also very different in diverse groups of countries that have had successful economic experiences based on the market—countries such as Japan and those of Scandinavia and southeast Asia. Similarly, there are profound differences concerning the role of the State among the European countries that pursue a socialized economy and others more oriented toward other types of market economies.

Latin American countries must redefine the State's role in the development of their societies according to their own situations, but always with the aim of placing the State at the service of greater economic efficiency and social equity.

Nevertheless, in the efforts to modernize the State and its institutions, several dilemmas persist for which recent experiences can provide some orientation or guidance. Thus, for example, few will still defend the compatibility of a highly interventionist State with the development strategies that have come to prevail in the region. However, those who maintain that the new economic policies do not require the guidance of a reduced but efficient State that is present in its areas of unavoidable responsibility are also in the minority. Between these two extremes, surely, lies not only the solution to the social question but also the general framework for economic activities and the preservation of market operations under conditions that prevent a concentration of economic power that would exclude the participation of all economic players. At issue, therefore, is not whether the State should be larger or smaller, but how we can have a State that is more efficient in carrying out the functions that are undeniably proper to it within the framework of current development strategies. I have already referred to the State's responsibility in maintaining macroeconomic equilibria and its role in the social sector; more could be done with respect to the part it plays in guiding economic reforms, transforming productive structures, and generally speaking, in modernizing our economies.

In carrying out these functions, the problems related to the size of the State, the decentralization of its activities, its efficiency, and its interaction with other economic and social players are but a few of the many other areas that still require a creative response appropriate to the various national situations. Nowadays there is widespread interest in reducing the size and sphere of the traditional State, ridding it of superfluous or unjustifiably costly responsibilities. This has spurred a vigorous process of privatization throughout the entire region. Naturally, this process cannot be carried out either dogmatically or unconscientiously. Appropriate criteria and techniques are necessary to make the efficient economic activity compatible with safeguarding the national patrimony and to ensure quality public monitoring of areas essential to the economic and social welfare of our countries.

The decentralization of the State, at the functional and geographical levels—regional, local, or municipal—has shown to be

Increased government efficiency

an indispensable tool in improving the effectiveness of public management and the allocation of resources for social expenditures. It has also proven to be a powerful instrument for mobilizing resources at the private or local level and a sound vehicle for the democratization and transparency of public operations through increased popular control. Clearly, however, this decentralization requires competence at every level in which it is established and a clear awareness of the potential and limitations of public spending.

Public and private interaction

Each country needs to define the supervisory, regulatory, productive, or social functions that it wishes to keep in the hands of the State. Each country must also define which spheres correspond primarily to the State and which to the private sector. Defining these areas and how they are to interact should tend to ensure economic efficiency and social equity and make them compatible with one another. What is unacceptable is for the State or the private sector to be able to act with impunity. To prevent this, the public apparatus must be made more professional, freeing it of political patronage. At the same time, the private sector must fully assume its economic and social responsibilities.

Strengthening the ability of private agents to act

The logical counterpart to State reform is the strengthening of the private sector. One of the factors that led to the adoption of the postwar Latin American development model was the weakness of private enterprise. Since then, the private sector has evolved considerably in Latin America. In the future, if the region's economies are to compete in an international market like we have today, private enterprise must assume a leadership role in expanding the region's productive forces and enhancing its international competitiveness. In this respect, medium-sized and small businesses, which in the past have had scant access to the usual sources of credit, technology, or trade, offer enormous possibilities. We have already identified one important area of potential in the microenterprise sector. It is necessary to reach these segments of the business sector through innovative programs that broaden the sectoral and geographical scope of normal enterprise support activities and through the greatest possible number of intermediaries.

Three basic conditions must be met for private enterprise to develop: first, clear and stable "rules of the game" must be established concerning the relationship between the State and private enterprise; second, a favorable investment climate must be created and maintained; and third, the relationship between labor and management must be reoriented through visionary and medium-term social pacts, based on closer ties between workers and the development of the enterprises that employ them.

State reform and the strengthening of the private sector go beyond the scope of these themes and point to the necessity of a complete reconstruction of our countries' institutional systems. Hence, together with concern about the above issues, there is a need to strengthen the various economic and social players that have a hand in development, apart from private enterprise, such as regional and local organizations, grassroots communities, professional associations, and other similar institutions.

Technological modernization

The development of the Latin American countries at the present time is closely linked to the nature and degree of their insertion into the international economy. We know that world trade in manufactures has expanded at a much faster rate than has total trade, and this difference is greater for products that contain a higher degree of technological innovation. Our countries' potential for producing competitively and penetrating world markets depends on their capacity to keep up with international technological trends and incorporate the new knowledge into the production of tradable goods and services. This, in turn, depends not only on the existence of programs designed specifically to promote scientific and technological development, but also on the organization of enterprise, on its relationship with the various productive sectors, on financial and marketing services, on the quality of the work force, and on the institutional, social, and political configuration of each country.

In this vein, the stability of relations within enterprises and among entrepreneurs, professionals, and workers, as well as the ability of these sectors to take concerted action that raises productivity are crucial for technological progress. This, in turn, is favored by the presence of organizations that bring these sectors together—

organizations whose legitimacy depends not only on their representativeness but also on their ability to foment the necessary accord.

Linkage with foreign investment sources and with multinational corporations can significantly help to incorporate foreign technology into the productive apparatus of Latin American countries and promote exports that are more technology-intensive. This link should be considered both a complement and a stimulus to the role of national private enterprise in its efforts to produce competitively and export to world markets.

Development of human resources

Incorporating modern technology into Latin America's economies cannot be achieved without an extraordinary effort to develop human resources. Here, as in the informal sector, problems like education and the development of human resources, once considered strictly from the social perspective, become key factors in economic development. The gap that Latin America must bridge in this area is determined on the one hand by the persistence of poverty and social inequality, and on the other by the demands created by the speed of productive and technological change. Undoubtedly, mobilizing resources toward education and human resource development is a problem; however, so is utilizing the resources allocated to these sectors more efficiently and in a manner that will produce the desired results.

Certainly, Latin America faces enormous problems associated with the quality of primary and secondary education, not to mention higher education and access to it. There is concern worldwide both about reforming education in line with the new demands of economic and social development and about the globalization of the economy; Latin America can neither shrug off nor put off this concern.

Modernization of technical training

The greatest bottleneck in human resource development, however, probably lies in technical and intermediate training programs. With so much of a demand for this type of training, it is counterproductive for the issue to remain pending. These programs must not only be intensified and brought up to date; they must be redesigned in order to link them more closely with the new job demands generated by Latin America's productive transformation.

Moreover, they must be given the broadest, most flexible foundation possible to provide workers with the basic skills necessary to manage in a rapidly evolving job market.

Hence, there is a need for these training programs to be integrated insofar as possible into the productive sectors, to be highly flexible, and to be targeted toward well-defined labor groups. Among these, of course, are groups associated with medium-sized and small businesses and the informal sector of the economy—those with the greatest deficiencies in this area. In addition, a special place should be assigned to programs aimed at training workers displaced from their traditional activities by rapid productive change.

To attend to the multiple needs of human resource development, flexible global strategies that integrate economic and social policy elements must be devised. Very close collaboration between the State and the private sector is also essential; while it is logical to expect the latter to make a major contribution to adapting human resources to its new requirements, past performance indicates that Latin America's private sectors have not always been in a position to do so. Hence, we see the importance of fostering greater interaction between the State and private enterprise.

Consolidating and expanding the integration processes

After a long, erratic, and somewhat unsuccessful trajectory, economic integration among the countries of the region has changed considerably and is beginning to play a very direct role in Latin America's new development strategies. One difference from those first attempts at integration is that today's efforts are generally more limited in scope with respect to the countries, sectors, and interests involved. At the same time, they are more flexible, more sensitive to market signals, and not defensive but competitive.

A new concept

A second feature is that countries that seek effective and complementary economic programs do so as a function of affinities that do not necessarily have anything to do with geographical proximity or similarities in per capita income; instead, they are concerned with the orientation, pace, and outcome of economic reforms, and with the comparative levels of productive competitiveness. A final difference that derives from this last point is that the latest attempts at integration and cooperation are highly oriented toward external relations with the rest of the world—that is, toward making the economies more able to participate in programs to export and penetrate the international markets.

Insofar as the new Latin American integration agreements retain these characteristics, they will play a decisive role in the development strategies throughout the region. A recent example of this lies perhaps in the agreements drawn up between Argentina and Brazil, with the adherence of Paraguay and Uruguay, and the founding of MERCOSUR. Likewise, the accords established this year between Chile and Mexico, and Chile and Venezuela are a very concrete indicator of these trends.

The crisis of the 1980s, together with the paralysis of the traditional integration schemes that, in any case, showed signs of exhaustion long ago, helped persuade the countries of the need to utilize integration and economic complementation to achieve greater exposure to international competition. Thus, countries that have recently shown an interest in promoting such agreements are very conscious of the need for their economies to meet certain basic requirements associated with their macroeconomic equilibria and productive competitiveness. Harmonizing economic policies takes on key importance if solid regional integration processes are to be sustained. In this context, an old problem of regional integration re-emerges with new vigor: the need for regional integration to rely on growing participation by the private sector in these initiatives and on bolstering intrasectoral investment among the different countries.

Integration and international competition

The international insertion of the region

There is widespread consensus that Latin American development strategies in the 1990s require greater economic openness and integration with the world economy. Toward this end, Latin American countries have instituted major reforms and have managed to expand their traditional and nontraditional exports considerably. In addition to appropriate macroeconomic policies in the areas of tariffs and exchange rates, policies in the form of fiscal incentives, technological support, and market information have been designed for specific sectors. Equally important are those that lift government restrictions that hamper exports, such as the maintenance of State-administered price systems. Latin American countries will have to continue along this path. These efforts, however, require concessions on the part of the international community, which still has not reciprocated the region's efforts, continues to enforce protectionist policies of every type, and has failed to come to the necessary agreements at the Uruguay Round of the GATT.

In this context, it is important to reconcile Latin America's interest in bolstering its ties to a world economy governed by clear trade regulations and a climate of fair competition, with the opportunities that are opening up on its own regional front. In addition to the advantages offered by the opening of trade in the midst of rising international competitiveness, in Latin America as in other parts of the world, new opportunities stemming from the current regional integration processes are unfolding. Such opportunities must not be perceived, however, as an alternative to vigorous participation in the world economy, but rather as a complement to it. Moreover, they must not be considered a defense against the complex dangers inherent in the current trend toward the formation of large regional economic blocs. Latin America, therefore, has a vital interest in the success of the Uruguay Round of the trade negotiations under the GATT.

Openness to competition

Nevertheless, opportunities unprecedented in scope and potential have recently opened up for Latin America under the economic and trade agreements provided for in the Enterprise for the Americas Initiative. The trade agreements between the United States, Canada, and Mexico constitute the most ambitious cooperative adventure in the economic history of the region. Moreover, these accords will stimulate a gradual extension of this type of scheme to agreements between the United States and other countries or groups of countries in the hemisphere. It should be stressed that progress in this direction will depend on solid economic performance and growing international competitiveness on the part of the countries of the region as a result of the intelligent and persistent application of the present economic reforms.

At the same time, far from precluding integration agreements among Latin American countries, the Enterprise for the Americas Initiative views such agreements as a requisite, insofar as these forms of association contribute to better economic policy management and increased productivity among the countries. The objectives of the Initiative and the creation of regional or subregional integration schemes are by no means mutually exclusive.

The environmental sustainability
of development

The world has come a long way from the Stockholm conference of 1971 to the meeting in Rio de Janeiro in June 1992. This trajectory has been impressive as far as Latin America is concerned. When the environmental issue emerged on a global scale in the early 1970s, the developing countries kept a certain distance from the industrialized nations, in the belief that their economic growth processes would necessarily put some degree of pressure on the environment. Twenty years later, the developing countries in general, and especially those of Latin America, have come to see the problem more clearly, and they have learned to balance the demands of development with respect for the environment without repeating the historical errors of the industrial world. The idea of ecologically sustainable economic development is beginning to gain ground and adherents.

In Latin America, the countries must undertake a productive transformation that, notwithstanding its vast reaches, will ensure the rational use of natural resources and the environment. It is not a question of curbing economic growth in the name of environmental preservation, though in the past, development was often achieved at a high environmental cost, especially through improper exploitation of natural resources. For Latin America, the challenge is not so much to improve the standard of living at the expense of the quality of life, but rather to raise the standard of living in an environmentally sustainable manner.

Concerning the link between development and the environment, major conceptual and perceptual changes have occurred. One of these is an awareness that the Earth's resources are limited and that a perverse process of destruction of these resources is under way throughout the world, including Latin America. Furthermore, there has been a growing consciousness of the importance of ecological problems common to all, such as the degradation of the air, the ozone layer, or the oceans. These are problems that can affect all of humanity, and thus, they are an inescapable issue for any country on the planet. Finally, beyond environmental protection policies, a close link has been discovered today between economic efficiency and the quality of the environment—of both the rural and urban habitat—of Latin American societies. Few problems will require greater public attention in the coming years than the environmental administration of the small and large urban centers of the region.

The political viability of current strategies

Economists cannot distance themselves from the political context of the development process, which presupposes social tranquility, democratic participation, and stable governments. The current political context for development is extraordinarily positive, marked as it is by transcendent processes of democratization. Ever-increasing political pluralism, social participation, and the search for broader consensus as the foundation for long-term governability are essential. Instituting economic reforms implies, among other things, moving from confrontation to rapprochement and consensus, and committing governments to basic political accords. Such agreements will make possible an acceptance of the changes, sacrifices, and time required for the reforms to bear fruit and permit their harmonization with democratic processes. In this case, technocratic solutions, while necessary, are not sufficient; we must recur to the art of politics.

The economic instability of our countries has often been responsible for their political vicissitudes. Recently, however, these vicissitudes have in many cases been at the root of economic instability. The profound process of economic and productive transformation that Latin America is now entering and the imperative of reinserting itself into the international market require political stability that can only be grounded in a new and very broad social contract. The scattering of political paths to the left and the right that occurred in Latin America after the basic consensus of the 1960s, which was characterized by moderate reformist regimes, marked the beginning of a return to middle-ground and practical positions, to the search for consensus instead of conflict, and to a more pragmatic and less ideological vision in the political sphere.

Political stability and economic development

It is relevant to note that in several countries, this trend has produced or is the inspiration behind initiatives leading to constitutional changes—changes that guarantee that moderation, stability, and the orderly transfer of power based on free elections will be key elements of the new political style. This is a very important task for the countries of the region and will deepen the institutional reforms that have helped make the political situation compatible with the economic situation.

History tells us that the type of great national consensus similar to the kind that must be bolstered today in Latin America, though not infrequently induced by the challenges of the external environment, has been the outcome of domestic political processes guided by visionary leadership.

Numerous Latin American thinkers have affirmed that, through tradition and culture, this part of the world has lived obsessed by the past. Moving beyond a development model responsible for regional growth during the postwar period and the painful crisis of the 1980s has obliged the countries to transcend the past with neither nostalgia nor complaints, and start building a future with a vision free of prejudices, a keen sense of reality, a creative spirit, and an irrevocable determination. This determination is the wellspring and support of the economic reforms under way.

This is why we state today that, far from looking toward the past, the countries of the region are continuing to strengthen structural reforms and the process of modernizing their economies. They must now take up the heavy burden imposed by their historical inheritance, and without delay undertake a profound social integration process that incorporates large marginal sectors into the distribution of the benefits that economic progress is beginning to produce. It is not just a question of an historical imperative born of a cultural heritage grounded in human dignity. It is also a need that stems from the very nature of the development strategy that our countries have adopted. At the same time, we must consolidate the new strategy of external openness and active insertion into the world economy and rest it upon the new integration processes that our national economies are undergoing.

The international cooperation agencies, above all those of the inter-American system—and most especially, the Inter-American Development Bank—cannot be less than their member countries and must therefore be prepared to contribute to this task.